10X 1/10 ✓ 5/12

Careers in Entertainment

Wayne Wilson

Mitchell Lane
PUBLISHERS

PO Box 619
Bear, Delaware 19701

Latinos at Work

Career Role Models for Young Adults

Careers in Community Service

Careers in Education

Careers in Entertainment

Careers in Law and Politics

Careers in the Music Industry

Careers in Publishing and Communications

Careers in Science and Medicine

Careers in Sports

Careers in Technology

Latino Entrepreneurs

Library of Congress Cataloging-In-Publication Data
Wilson, Wayne, 1953-.
     Careers in entertainment/Wayne Wilson.
          p. cm.—(Latinos at work)
     Includes bibliographical references and index.
     ISBN 1-58415-083-1
     1. Performing arts—Vocational guidance—United States—Juvenile
literature 2.Hispanic Americans in the performing arts—Juvenile
literature. I. Title. II. Series.
PN1580.W55 2000
791'.023'73—dc21   2001038089

Careers in Entertainment

About the Author

Wayne Wilson was born and raised in Los Angeles. He received a Master of Arts in Education from the University of California, Los Angeles. For 16 years he was co-owner and president of a pioneering and innovative publishing company specializing in multicultural designs. Recently he completed interviews with influential Latino men throughout the country and wrote over 160 biographies for *Encuentros: Hombre A Hombre*, a comprehensive vocational education book to be published by the California Department of Education. Several of Wilson's short stories have been published in commercial and literary magazines. Wilson lives in Venice Beach, California with his wife and daughter and is currently working on his first novel and screenplay.

Photo Credits

All photographs were courtesy of the persons being profiled.

Acknowledgments

The profiles of success depicted in Part Two were all written from the author's personal interviews. Interviews were conducted as follows: Rey Villalobas-1999 interview, updated in 2/01; Gregory Nava-1999 interview, updated 2/01; Moctesuma Esparza-7/31/00; Dennis Leoni- 8/16/01; Bill Melendez- 4/11/01; George Lopez- 4/13/01; Maria Jimenez Henley- 4/10/01; Emanuel Nuñez- 4/11 and 4/28/01; Bel Hernandez- 4/9/01; Severo Perez- 1999, update interview 1/01.

Publisher's Note

The careers depicted in this series are by no means all-inclusive. We have tried to show a representation of what is available by industry. Your career center at school or your local library can be of additional help identifying careers we might not have covered. The Web sites mentioned in this book were all active as of the publication date. Because of the fleeting nature of Web enterprises, we cannot guarantee that all sites will be operational when you are reading this book.

Contents

Part 1
Choosing a Career in Entertainment   8

Part 2
Profiles of Success   34

Part 3
Resources   84

Indexes   92

Bill Melendez and Charles Schulz worked together for 44 years creating a library of Peanuts programming, including 63 half-hour specials, 5 one-hour specials, 4 feature films, and 372 commercials.

P A R T 1

Choosing a Career in Entertainment

TABLE OF CONTENTS

Actor/Actress	14	Film Editor	26
Advertising Copywriter	14	Journalist, Entertainment	26
Agent	16	Lighting Designer (Theater)	27
Animator	16	Makeup Artist	27
Art Director/Production Designer	17	Playwright	28
Attorney, Entertainment	17	Press Agent, Personal	28
Casting Director	17	Press Agent, Theatrical	29
Choreographer	18	Producer	29
Cinematographer	18	Public Relations and Promotional Director	30
Comedian	21	Scenic Designer (Theater)	30
Comedy Writer	21	Screenwriter	30
Community Affairs Director (TV)	22	Set Designer	31
Composer	22	Sound Editor	31
Costume Designer	23	Stage Director (Theater)	32
Critic/Reviewer (Print Media)	23	Stage Manager (Theater)	32
Critic/Reviewer (TV/Radio)	23	Tour Publicist	32
Director (Feature Films)	25	Unit Publicist	33
Director (Television)	25		

The presence of Latinos in Hollywood, both in front of and behind the camera, still has a long way to go, but things appear to be changing with the rising stars of actors such as Jennifer Lopez, Freddie Prinze, Jr., Penelope Cruz, Benecio Del Toro, Benjamin Bratt, Cameron Diaz, and Salma Hayek. "We've made tremendous strides," Luis Reyes told *The Los Angeles Times* in 2000. Reyes, with Peter Rubie, cowrote the book *Hispanics in Hollywood,* which contains over 7,500 entries describing Latino-themed movies, TV shows, and biographies of Latinos in the entertainment industry. He said that between the first (1994) and second (2000) editions of his book, he has noticed a "burst of activity" in regard to the casting of Latino actors and Latino-themed projects.

In March 2001, Benecio Del Toro was awarded a Golden Globe and an Oscar as Best Supporting Actor for his role in *Traffic.* And, despite the usual shortsightedness of power brokers in the television and film business, some Latinos were even getting cast in roles that could go to actors of any color. For example, Jennifer Lopez was cast in *Out of Sight* and *The Wedding Planner,* and

Jessica Alba was cast in James Cameron's *Dark Angel. The Wedding Planner* and *Spy Kids,* a family adventure film by Robert Rodriguez and starring Antonio Banderas, were both at the top of the box office charts in 2001.

On cable television there is *Resurrection Blvd.,* with a stellar cast of Latino actors, produced by Dennis Leoni. A new face in the spotlight is Tessie Santiago, who stars in the syndicated series *Queen of Swords* as the horse-riding, sword-wielding, masked heroine Tessa Alvarado. In addition, work for actors on and behind the scenes became even more promising with Gregory Nava's multi-picture deal with New Line Cinema. Along with the growth of Latinos in the entertainment industry emerged a trade publication called *Latin Heat,* whose specific purpose is to cover Latinos in television, film, music, and theater. The magazine was developed partly as a result of studies identifying Latinos as the number one moviegoing audience.

On the surface it seems that Latinos are finally turning heads in Hollywood and that with each individual success, better roles will be offered. However, many experts adamantly contend that although the job prospects in the entertainment industry may appear to be getting better, Latinos are a long way from being in the mainstream of the entertainment industry. Veterans in the field warn aspiring Latino performers to approach this situation with guarded optimism.

Even though Hollywood is starting to respond, the progress has been very slow. Rita Moreno won an Oscar in 1961 for her role as Anita in *West Side Story,* but she was disheartened by the lack of quality roles offered to her after her groundbreaking performance. From the 1950s even to the present there continue to be stereotypical images of Latinos, ranging from drug dealers, gang members, Latin lovers, hookers, and maids. Few actors in the United States during this period have been able to break through these stereotypes and play leading characters in complex roles. Some of them are Raul Julia, Sonia Braga, Jimmy Smits, Edward James Olmos, Hector Elizando, and Elizabeth Peña.

An American Family by Greg Nava, which boasts an all-star cast of Latino actors, was praised by critics such as Howard Rosenberg of *The Los Angeles Times.* Nava had high hopes for the program because it would have been the first Latino family drama in the history of network television. He was devastated when the television pilot, made in 2000 for CBS, was not selected for that season's prime-time lineup. Undaunted, Nava continued to shop the show around. It took a year to find the program a new home with the smaller PBS network. Still, though it may not have the budget of a major network, Nava says optimistically, "PBS will be seen as a boutique showcase for *American Family.*"

In 1991 a report commissioned by the Screen Actors Guild (SAG) and compiled by the Tomás Rivera Policy Institute—titled "Missing in Action: Latinos In and Out of Hollywood"—stated that Hispanic actors comprised just 4 percent of the guild's membership and received only 3.5 percent of guild roles. And this was a 72 percent increase from 1992. Furthermore, Hispanics accounted for less than 2 percent of Writers Guild of America (WGA) West members. A coauthor of the SAG report, Harry Pachon, who is president of the Tomás Rivera Policy Institute and professor at Pitzer College/Claremont Graduate University in Claremont, California, says, "There are, of course, notable exceptions, but by and large the industry continues to overlook Hispanics." A study released in 1994 by the Center for Media and Public Affairs posited that Latinos are faring far worse in today's TV climate than they were during the *I Love Lucy* days when maverick Desi Arnaz starred in and produced the show.

The SAG report revealed that old stereotypes and a lack of understanding of Hispanic social, economic, and cultural diversity are the main reasons that Latinos are one of the most underrepresented ethnic groups in feature films, television, theater, and other entertainment. Industry executives admitted in the report that they tended to see Hispanics as only dark-skinned immigrants who speak with a heavy accent. Most seemed unable to view Latinos as a group defined by language and country of origin. Studio executives stated that economics determined what they produced, and they felt that Latino movies and television programs would not succeed financially. The executives did not think Latino actors had enough star power to draw large audiences to the box office.

We can be grateful for advocacy groups such the National Hispanic Media Coalition, which in 1995 waged a full-scale attack on the ABC network, its affiliates, and its major advertisers for not creating more positive TV roles for Latino characters; and the National Council of La Raza, which staged a "brown out" in 1999 to protest a lack of Latinos on network TV. These groups helped voice the concerns of the Hispanic population about having more shows that demonstrate a more realistic, varied, and positive portrayal of the Latin population.

The battle for a greater inclusion of Hispanics into the film business has involved not only protests, but also Latinos' taking positive steps and recognizing their own achievements and successes. In 1994 the National Council of La Raza created the American Latino Media Arts (ALMA) Awards to honor positive portrayals of Latinos and their outstanding artistic achievement in film, television, and music. The 2001 ALMA Awards honored Jennifer Lopez as Entertainer of the Year, and Nickelodeon earned accolades for promoting cultural diversity in children's programming. Other winners included Carlos Avila, Elizabeth Peña, Martin Sheen, Ruben Blades, Lauren Velez, Gina Torres, Joe Menendez, Felix Alcala, A. Martinez, Saundra Santiago, John Leguizamo,

Bill Melendez, Geraldo Rivera, *Resurrection Blvd., For Love of Country: The Arturo Sandoval Story,* and more.

Demographics prove that Latinos are the fastest-growing minority in the United States. By the year 2004 it is projected that Hispanics will be the largest minority in the country. Latinos are entering the labor market at faster rates than non-Latinos due to higher birth rates and continued immigration.

Latinos currently represent 11 percent of the U.S. population, yet they are the most underrepresented ethnic group on television and in film; their representation in these media outlets constitute less than one-third of their real portion of the population. On the other hand, Latinos have demonstrated a buying power of more than $340 billion, and since it is advertising revenue that makes or breaks television programs, Latinos are making their voices heard. The Latino influence in America is growing both economically and culturally, and the media industry cannot continue to ignore it.

In 1996 Jose Luis Ruiz, the executive director of the National Latino Communications Center, a nonprofit production company, told *Frontera Magazine,* "Latinos have a long way to go before their roles in TV sitcoms reflect their roles in real life. Until ABC, CBS, NBC, Fox, and Warner Bros. begin to feel that economic push in the right direction, it's up to us to keep nurturing talented young Latino writers, directors, producers, and actors with training programs."

The tremendous growth of Hispanics in the United States has produced a growing demand for entertainment alternatives. Hispanics are requesting more Latin radio stations, music, theater offerings, television shows, and movies that accurately express the breadth of the Latino experience. The greater the demand, the more opportunities become available. There is no question that the first network to successfully launch a Hispanic sitcom will capitalize on an enormous TV market share that has impacting spending power.

Already the job prospects for radio, television, and film are expected to grow between now and the year 2006 as new stations are licensed and the number of cable systems continues to rise. Those individuals pursuing a career in entertainment will be encouraged by a recent statement made by veteran television and movie producer

Moctesuma Esparza to *The Los Angeles Times:* "There is, in fact, a critical mass of Latinos forming in the industry. The numbers are just coming to a point where people are just beginning to feel like there is a community. This extraordinary wave of Latino celebrity and acceptance that is occurring now is not only our present, it represents a wonderful future. The issue here is not how to make every single movie a crossover success. The fact is that we are now arriving at a time and place where all of the possibilities to succeed are real and no longer pipe dreams."

The entertainment industry provides a variety of jobs for ambitious, creative, talented, skilled, educated, and resourceful people who are well prepared in the areas of writing, editing, acting, directing, producing, cinematography, law, animation, management, costume design, makeup, and more.

You will find that for many of the careers highlighted in this book, preferred applicants have a degree in theater arts, communications, speech, art, engineering, public relations, design, business, or other related fields. It is not always necessary, but in this competitive society a degree may give you that extra edge, as well as the opportunity to establish contacts.

Experience is also important, and you may find that the best way to gain experience is through an apprenticeship or internship program. Many of these programs do not offer a salary, but what you will gain in knowledge will be invaluable if you are pursuing a career in a specific field. Second, there exist special programs that are dedicated to providing training opportunities to Latinos and other minorities in media careers.

This book will help you explore some of the career opportunities that may await you in the world of entertainment. It will provide you with an overview of the field, but it is in no way an exhaustive compilation of all the careers that are available to you. It is simply a way of making you aware of your options and pointing you in the right direction.

Dr. Miquela Rivera, in her *Minority Career Book*, says, "To reach the winner's circle, you need to be prepared, focus your direction, and stick with your plans."

Careers in Entertainment will help prepare you by giving you information on a multitude of interesting careers.

Remember, as a Latino, you have the opportunity to bring a wealth of personal experiences and resources into your chosen profession. Keep this in mind as you review the alphabetized list of careers in Part One. Furthermore, Part One discusses what type of qualities employers look for in a candidate. It gives data on the education and training you will need, as well as what salary you can expect to earn. Also included are brief real-life stories of Latinos currently working in the entertainment field.

Part Two tells more in-depth stories about people who have been successful in the entertainment field. Each profile will offer a firsthand account of how this individual achieved success in his or her respective career. You will read about Latinos who have overcome major obstacles to realize their dreams. By reading many of these stories, you will find that successful people aren't working simply for the money, they are working because they love what they do.

And finally, in Part Three you will find a comprehensive list of resources—including books and directories, professional organizations and associations, internships, service programs, and Internet sources—to help you delve deeper into specific careers.

The entertainment industry is crying out for more voices that reflect our multicultural society—voices that may showcase the depth and beauty of Hispanic culture. But those voices cannot be heard unless Latinos acquire the education and skills to go after these jobs. These are the best and worst of times for Latinos in the entertainment industry; even though they are better represented today, Latinos are still terribly underrepresented in the industry, and there is no guarantee this will change. But there are positive signs that things are better for Latinos in this field than they have ever been before.

From the inception of film, there have been Latinos who have blazed a path for others to follow. As the door creaks open a little wider from the success of today's Latin stars, we hope to see greater and continued opportunities for those Latinos pursuing a career in this field. But it cannot happen unless you take the first steps toward educating yourself about the industry. And, if establishing a career in the entertainment industry is what you truly want to do, then you know it will take persistence, hard work, and determination. The choice is yours. Good luck!

Selected Job Descriptions in Entertainment

Actor/Actress

Actors perform roles for radio, commercials, cartoons, television, and feature films. The production may be a drama, musical, or comedy and require the actor to tell a story by communicating through his or her speech and (except for cartoons) body language. Or the production may be animated, in which case the actor must perform voice-overs. Before an actor appears before a camera or an audience, he or she must study the script, analyze the characters, memorize the lines, and have a thorough understanding of the director's viewpoint regarding the story. Frequently an actor has to research a particular role, which may require that he or she observe a real-life counterpart.

Although acting is regarded as a glamorous profession, very few actors or actresses achieve star status. A large number become experienced professionals who are cast in supporting roles on stage and in television and motion pictures. The actor's life is often filled with uncertainty, anxiety, unemployment, humiliating auditions, and numerous rejections, sometimes based on things beyond the actor's control, such as height or even skin color. Those who succeed usually love the acting profession and demonstrate the versatility, patience, hard work, dedication, humility, and commitment it takes to rise above adversity.

According to Actor's Equity studies, the weekly minimum salary for an actor under contract is $1,180. The average income members of the Screen Actors Guild earn for acting is reported as less than $5,000 a year. Extras earn about $100 to $200 per film. Of course, superstars earn millions.

Advertising Copywriter

The primary responsibility of all advertising copywriters is to develop copy for ads. In radio and television they must be able to create concepts for advertisements in addition to producing them and getting them on the air. Copywriters need to be able to write clearly and concisely and in a variety of styles. The copy is usually spoken by an announcer or actor, so the words must be easy to understand and articulate.

Rita Moreno-Groundbreaking Latina Actress

Rita Moreno is the only female performer to have won four of the entertainment industry's top honors: an Oscar for her role in *West Side Story,* Emmys for her appearances on *Rockford Files* and *The Muppet Show,* a Tony as Googie Gomez in *The Ritz,* and a Grammy for *The Electric Company Album.* In 1979 this accomplishment was entered into the *Guinness Book of World Records.*

This pioneering stage and screen actress was born Rosa Delores Alverio on December 11, 1931, in Humacao, Puerto Rico. After her parents divorced, she and her mother moved to New York City. Rosa was five years old. Her natural talents already visible at an early age, upon the suggestion of a friend, Rosa was enrolled in Spanish dance classes with gifted teacher Paco Cansino.

She landed her first part on Broadway at the age of 13 and her first film role six years later, in 1950. Typecast as the stereotypical Latin in her early movies, in 1961 she catapulted to stardom playing Anita in the screen version of *West Side Story.* Despite winning an Oscar for Best Supporting Actress, Hollywood remained shortsighted. Undeterred, the versatile actress appeared in various productions throughout Europe and the United States.

Among numerous prestigious awards, in 1990 Rita Moreno was honored with the Hispanic Heritage Award. A humanitarian and strong civil rights activist, Moreno consistently makes contributions to the arts and to the Latino community. Full of boundless energy, she has released an exercise video and still performs her one-woman stage show.

Her film and television credits include *Pagan Love Song; Singin' in the Rain; Garden of Evil; The King and I; The Deerslayer; The Night of the Following Day; Carnal Knowledge; The Ritz; The Four Seasons; Happy Birthday, Gemini; Nine To Five; Evita Peron;* and currently the hit HBO series *OZ.*

Most radio and television stations recommend obtaining a bachelor's degree in journalism, communications, English, or a related field. The annual salary for an advertising copywriter ranges from $18,000 to over $75,000.

Agent

Agents may represent athletes, models, performers, writers, directors, cinematographers, and others. An agent acts as a representative and advocate for his or her clients in the entertainment industry. An agents' primary responsibility is to obtain work for their clients. In doing so, agents must strategize and brainstorm ideas with them. They develop a career plan for their clients and negotiate deals with production studios. In some cases, agents make deals by assembling several clients, such as an actor, director, and writer, on one film, which is called packaging the movie.

A bachelor's degree and experience working in an agency is preferred. Agents need to be creative, business-oriented, skilled negotiators, and articulate, and they must enjoy working with people. It also helps for an agent to be knowledgeable about law, particularly in the area of contracts and copyrights. Some agents work out of large lavish offices that service hundreds of clients; others work out of small offices, a few even out of their cars. Since an agent won't survive if their client is not successful, they often act as advisers and will do everything they can to enhance the capabilities of the client they represent. This is tough work and fiercely competitive, but the earnings are potentially unlimited. Agents earn at least 10 percent of their clients' salaries.

Animator

An animator is a visual artist who is responsible for drawing by hand or with the assistance of computers the animated cartoons seen on television and in the movies. Companies such as the Walt Disney Corporation, Warner Brothers, Hanna-Barbera, and others employ a large number of animators. In many large corporations animators work as a team and have areas of specialization. An animator may be responsible for drawing a specific character, scene, background layout, color pattern, or sequence. The various pieces are then assembled into one cartoon.

The position does not require a degree, but having a bachelor's degree in graphic design or fine arts is certainly beneficial. Above all an animator must be creative and have excellent drawing skills. It is also highly recommended that a person take classes in computer skills and computer animation. Annual earnings are $18,000 to over $55,000.

Art Director/Production Designer

The person responsible for the overall look and design of a feature film or television show is called the art director or production designer. In order to determine what visual elements to develop, the production designer works closely with the director, as well as with the cinematographer and costume designer. The creative team under the production designer's supervision produces drawings, models, and plans for the director's approval, and those images are translated into sets and locations. Since the production designer is usually in charge of a large staff and budget, he or she must also report to the producer.

A production designer often has to work long hours on a project, and it can be both mentally and physically draining. Experienced production designers report that a broad liberal arts education and strong technical knowledge will allow a person to accomplish more in this position. Production designers earn a weekly minimum of about $1,800.

Attorney, Entertainment

The specialized practice of law for the entertainment industry is in the film and television arena. Entertainment attorneys are often employed by large firms, but some operate independent practices. The entertainment attorney is the legal representative or counsel for writers, actors, producers, directors, and others in the film industry. This person negotiates the terms of clients' contracts with studios and producers. An entertainment attorney does not, however, initiate contracts for his or her clients; this is the job of the agent.

Successful entertainment attorneys must have a strong law background, a great business sense, and a love, understanding, and protectiveness for the creative arts. The starting salary for an entertainment attorney is around $75,000 per year.

Casting Director

A casting director auditions and interviews performers for specific parts in a play, television show, or movie. To match the right person with a certain part, a casting director must read the script and then meet with the producer and director to get their perspective on how the picture should be cast. After the meeting, the casting director prepares a cast breakdown, which is a description of each role. Once this is approved by the producer and director, the casting director begins his or her search for the right people.

If the casting director has a specific actor or actress in mind for the part, he or she will contact the actor's agent to check out interest and availability, and then set up an appointment. Many times well-known actors will get a role without an audition.

Salary for a casting director varies. Much of it depends on the size and quality of the production, the budget, and how well known the casting director is in the industry. An apprenticeship or internship in this field is highly recommended.

Choreographer

A choreographer is responsible for designing the movements that go with the music or mood of a particular show or dance production. Choreographers must have an active imagination and be able to create new dances or adapt existing dances and integrate them into a specific production. A choreographer must be able to assess what a human body can do and use that knowledge to teach dancers how to move in a dance performance. But this person must possess more than just a knowledge of dance and music. The choreographer also needs to have expertise in costuming, lighting, and staging.

Although a degree is helpful, many choreographers are self-taught. They draw from their own experiences and watch other choreographers at work. Many have had years of ballet and other dance education and experience. Earnings from fee and performance royalties, depending on the size and prestige of the production, range from $500 a week to six figures or more a year.

Cinematographer (Director of Photography)

Everything related to the lighting and camera work on a motion picture is usually handled by the cinematographer. A cinematographer (or director of photography—DP) begins his or her job by carefully reading a script so that he or she can ascertain the mood of the film. He or she will also work very closely with the director to develop an overall concept for the film. Once this has been determined, it becomes the responsibility of the DP to use his or her artistic vision to set the vision of the director onto film. A cinematographer will watch the director rehearse

Do You Have What it Takes to be a Cinematographer?-Advice from Reynaldo Villalobos

Rey Villalobos is one of the most sought after directors of photography in Hollywood. He has worked on over 40 feature films and television productions as a cinematographer or director. As a cinematographer, he says, "Anything you see on my films, is what I've done. I've put the lighting in, whether it's dark or bright or interesting, whatever." He further explains that as a director, he has to pick the shots, choose the angles, meet with his cameramen, and discuss the material with the actors to clarify what they are expected to do in their roles.

Rey never attended film school, but the movies he has enhanced with his visual dynamics have been a topic of discussion in many a film class. Determined to work from the ground up, Villalobos started delivering equipment for a film house. In fact, he did all types of jobs for the company, working as a laborer, painter, and then as an assistant doing film titles. He found out very early in his profession that he couldn't sit back and wait for someone to do something for him, he'd have to do it himself. "I've always had to create my own way," Villalobos says proudly. "People may tell you how good you are, that you're the greatest! You're the best! But no one does anything for you—you have to do it!"

Although Villalobos gained much of his knowledge from on-the-job training, he encourages people interested in a film career to get good grades in high school so that they can go to college and study film, photography, directing, or production. He also stresses that while they're in school they should try to establish contacts in the film and television industry. "While you're in school, you've got to go to all the studios and meet people and offer to come in and help them. Tell them, 'You don't even have to pay me for it.' You learn by volunteering."

The final advice that Villalobos offers to young people is this: "Believe in yourself and don't let anybody else tell you who you are."

Meet Comedian John Leguizamo

Born in 1965, versatile entertainer John Leguizamo is the son of Colombian immigrants. His parents came to New York in 1966, leaving John and his baby brother, Sergio, in Bogotá with their grandparents. A year later the boys joined their parents in New York and the family settled in Queens.

John Leguizamo experienced a very troubled childhood, filled with poverty, a strict and hypercritical father, the divorce of his parents, difficulty in school, and petty arrests. Despite being raised in such a stressful environment, Leguizamo can remember watching such TV shows as *Flip Wilson, Carol Burnett,* and *I Love Lucy.* He'd dance along with *Soul Train.* His antics would make his parents laugh, and the tensions would suddenly lift.

This self-described misfit turned his life around when he focused on acting and stand-up comedy. In an interview with *Parade Magazine* he said, "Without acting, I would have ended up somewhere really messed up. The fact I made it was like a miracle."

Leguizamo has starred in more than 20 films, including *Casualties of War; Hangin' With the Homeboys; Carlito's Way; To Wong Fu, Thanks for Everything Julie Newmar; The Fan; Romeo & Juliet; Spawn; Summer of Sam;* and *Super Mario Bros.* He stars as Henri de Toulouse-Lautrec in his most recent film, *Moulin Rogue.* The actor has also earned critical acclaim and prestigious awards for his three one-man stage shows, *Mambo Mouth,* 1990; *Spic-O-Rama,* 1992; and *Freak,* 1998. *Freak* was based on his memories of his family and other immigrants in New York City. The play ran for nearly six months to sold-out houses on Broadway and earned Tony nominations for Best Actor and Best Play. Leguizamo also narrates the childhood excursions of Larry, the youngest Garcia brother on *The Brothers Garcia,* a live-action family sitcom with an all-Latino cast and team of writers, directors, and producers.

the actors before designing the lighting and organizing the details of the photography.

The cinematographer must be able to balance an artistic sensibility with technology. He or she must demonstrate a concern with framing, lighting, style, composition, continuity, and exposure. A skillful cinematographer can create magical worlds of romance or harsh futuristic environments with the right lighting, focus, and camera angles. Creating such imaginative worlds requires that the DP have creative planning meetings with set and costume designers, because the sets and colors have an immediate impact on the cinematographer's work.

Salaries for this position vary widely. In television a DP earns a minimum of $2,500 per week. Renowned cinematographers can earn $15,000 or more per week in movies. They are also able to earn excellent salaries making corporate videos and commercials.

Comedian

A comedian's job is to make people laugh. Comedians do this by performing monologues or skits, telling jokes, singing funny songs, impersonating famous people, performing comedic dances, wearing funny costumes, contorting their face, and so on.

Stand-up comedians work in nightclubs and entertain audiences with jokes, one-liners, impressions, and humorous stories. If his or her act is truly sharp, a comedian may be asked to appear on a television talk show or comedy special. This may eventually provide the opportunity for this person to have his or her own television series or even a movie role.

Comedians often write their own material, and sometimes they write material for other comedians. Writing humor does not require having a formal degree, and comedians come from all walks of life. However, comedians usually walk a long path to success: traveling and working in dingy nightclubs in front of only a few people on their way to larger and larger gigs.

Earnings range from $150 to over $20,000 per week, depending on the level of popularity and stardom. If you can consistently make an audience laugh, you will be richly rewarded.

Comedy Writer

Some of the funniest lines delivered by our favorite comedians were written by comedy writers. Sometimes the comedy writer may also be a comic. Comedy writers develop humorous material that includes skits, jokes, gags, song parodies, amusing speeches, and more. Many write not only for comedians, but also for entertainers, television shows, business or industry functions, and publications.

There is no formal training to be a comedy writer. However, you can find classes and seminars that offer comedy writing. The annual earnings for a comedy writer vary widely. Depending on the type of comedy and the professional reputation of the person for whom it is written, you can earn from $20,000 to over $150,000 per year.

Community Affairs Director (Television)

A community affairs director is largely responsible for developing, writing, and producing public service announcements and programs that cover events in the community. Of course, the number of duties depends on the size of the station. Shows may be presented in a variety of formats, such as a talk show panel or a documentary. Public service announcements might focus on warnings about drinking and driving, gangs, or teen sex; on community meetings; or on the importance of prenatal care. In addition, community affairs direc-

tors often meet with various nonprofit and civic organizations and plan social service events sponsored by their station.

A bachelor's degree is usually required. Excellent writing and verbal skills are important. Earnings vary depending on the director's experience; they can range from $20,000 to $55,000 or more per year.

Composer

Feature films, television shows, and theater productions have given us some of our most popular and memorable music. Today, songs from a movie's sound track may be released before you've even seen a single trailer. If the sound track becomes a hit, it may generate even more interest for the film. The major challenge for a film composer is to be able to meld original music with the screen's images. A film composer must have tremendous musical abilities with the unique gift of being able to actualize a director's vision in musical language. Usually the composer begins his or her work in postproduction, writing the music and orchestrating the score.

Film composition is a difficult field to break into, but producers are always searching for a "new sound." The best opportunities may be available in television, because there are so many shows on the air. Salaries vary depending upon whether the project is a high- or low-budget film. Composers can make from a few thousand dollars to over $200,000 per film.

Costume Designer

The costume designer is responsible for designing all the outfits and accessories for the cast of a theater production, television show, or movie. The costume designer must first read the script and decide the type and number of costumes needed for a particular show. Costume designers give an ambiance to a production and help bring the characters to life through the choice of costumes. Sometimes this may entail doing research on the specific time period in which the show or film is set so that the costumes will match. The clothes can be developed from an original design or purchased or rented. Costume designer Sylvia Vega-Vasquez has designed a wide spectrum of clothing to fit the diverse personalities of the Santiagos on Showtime's *Resurrection Blvd.* The clothes range from Beverly Hills chic to East Los Angeles nouveau styles.

A bachelor's degree in fashion, costume design, theater arts, or a related field is preferred in this industry. The amount of your earnings depends on whether you are in a union or not. Payment ranges from $500 to over $100,000 per production.

Critic/Reviewer (Print Media)

Critics who work in the print media (newspapers and magazines) write reviews for feature films, plays, television shows, concerts, music albums, and other forms of entertainment. When critics attend the opening of a play or new movie, the key ingredient in their writing is objectivity. They must remain objective while writing a review on the quality of a production or an actor's performance. Some critics, particularly those who write for larger publications, are more specialized in particular areas such as music, movies, theater, or opera. These specialists are highly knowledgeable about their specific medium. Annual earnings of a critic working in the print media range from $15,000 to over $65,000. A bachelor's degree is recommended.

Critic/Reviewer (Television/Radio)

Those critics who work in the broadcasting industry review theatrical pro-

Severo Perez-On Being an Independent Filmmaker

A prodigious writer, director, and producer, Perez has been in the film business since 1972 and has produced hundreds of films and videos, ranging from three-second animated clips to feature films. Most of Perez's work has been independent of Hollywood. He prefers to initiate and produce his own projects—to conceive, write, produce, raise money, and direct them. This award-winning filmmaker has covered topics such as the Tuskegee Airmen, integration, AIDS, the impact of immigration, writing, biographies, the Battle of the Alamo, and much more.

Perez never went to film school, and people questioned how this Mexican American was qualified to make movies. There was some resentment from his peers, particularly his white peers, in the beginning. "I guess I'm my father's son. I wasn't going to let anybody beat me, or be more together or more prepared. I really believe you win people's respect by proving yourself. But it has to be a two-way street—they have to prove themselves to you, too! Ultimately many of the people I started off with in the business dropped out because they never created their own breaks."

Perez believes that some of the greatest traits you can have as a filmmaker are determination and an absolute belief in what you are doing. He goes on to say: "First of all you must believe that the idea you are pursuing is worth the effort and stick with it till you see it to the end, because along the way there will be many fingers poking at it.

"The most important part is that you have to believe in yourself and believe in the creative process and learn about your own creative process. You can learn to make movies in six weeks. You don't have to get a master's degree or a doctorate to learn how to operate the camera . . . but the part that you can't learn is the part that comes from inside. The thing that makes a movie great is that it comes from an individual vision that is achieved."

ductions, concerts, symphonies, movies, television shows, and music. They attend plays, movie screenings, or concerts, or they may view television shows or listen to music at home before writing a review and reading it over the air. During a televised review the critic may show a clip of the particular show being covered. The critic must exercise honesty and objectivity when reviewing an actor's performance or critiquing a production. Sometimes critics assign ratings to productions to indicate how good they think they are.

The job requires exceptional writing skills, the ability to work under tight deadlines, and a good speaking voice. A bachelor's degree and experience working in journalism or broadcasting is preferred. Depending on the station's size, location, and market, a critic can earn anywhere from $18,000 to $100,000 or more a year.

Director (Feature Films)

The director of a motion picture is the artistic leader of the production team and is responsible for every decision that shapes the film. The director collaborates with his or her creative team, which includes the screenwriter, producer, cinematographer, editor, and costume designer. He or she may also assist the producer with scheduling, casting, scouting locations, budgeting, and hiring the film crew. Prior to shooting the film, the director meets with the cinematographer to discuss the look of the film. Once the filming starts, the director rehearses the actors and shoots the film.

After the filming, the director reviews the "dailies" with the film editor to select the best takes, then begins assembling the film, which may take weeks or months of cutting and editing scenes. During postproduction, other specialists the director meets with include the composer for the movie's music, the sound editor to help fine-tune the background noise for each scene, and the marketing specialists to provide assistance with the creation of the movie trailer.

A highly competitive field, the average pay for a director ranges from $6,000 to over $10,000 for every week worked. In feature films, a director's salary is heavily dependent on the film's budget. Major studios often pay well-known directors millions.

Director (Television)

A television director is responsible for all decisions pertaining to a television program. These programs may range from local newscasts to game shows, sitcoms, one-hour dramas, musicals, and made-for-TV movies. The director sets the tone and overall quality of the show. To achieve the type of mood he or she is looking for requires supervising and organizing the work of actors, screenwriters, lighting and sound technicians, camera operators, editors, and other personnel. The entire production crew relies on the director to be a leader and to make good decisions.

Working as a director often entails a great deal of stress. Directors are responsible for pulling together all the elements that make for a great production. A director must be a good listener, adaptable, focused, and able to block out any distractions to pulling together a great program, broadcast, or film.

Recently the Director's Guild Association has made stronger efforts to promote the hiring of minorities and women. Annual earnings for directors range from $28,000 to over $120,000.

Film Editor

Once the film crew has completed its work and left the set, the film goes into postproduction. The most important responsibility of the film editors—to make sure a film realizes its full potential—comes into play at this time. Film editors work closely with the film director to sift through the film and choose the best shots and images. They polish each scene to make sure that the best work during production is captured on screen. A film editor not only makes cuts, he or she also adds scenes or rearranges them for the sake of continuity and a smooth flow. Editing can be a complex job that may take weeks to finish, but a skilled film editor can make a good film great.

Film editing is difficult to break into. Salaries vary. Professional editors can earn $6,000 to $8,000 per week. The basic salary for film editors is about $30 per hour. An editorial apprentice can earn about $22 an hour, and an assistant editor about $25 per hour.

Journalist, Entertainment

Entertainment journalists write about all facets of the entertainment industry, including celebrity news, special events, and performances. Some journalists focus on a specialized area of entertainment such as music, theater, television, or feature films. Entertainment journalists often receive press kits, biographies, news releases, and celebrity photographs from press agents and publicists to enhance their feature articles.

Like any journalism career, this job requires gathering information through interviews, tips, leads, and research. Moreover, an entertainment journalist looks for an interesting angle when writing about a particular subject. These journalists must attend press conferences, opening parties, and entertainment events for their reviews or articles. In some cases a journalist may have to take photographs to go with their story. A bachelor's degree in journalism or a related field is preferred. Earnings range from $15,000 to $100,000 or more annually.

Lighting Designer (Theater)

The person responsible for all the lighting of a play or other theatrical production is known as the lighting designer. He or she must organize all the technical aspects as well as the artistic design. A lighting designer meets with the producer, director, and scenic designer to help establish the tone and mood of a particular stage show. How an audience knows the time of day on a stage or views cast members' expressions and movements is determined by the lighting effect of the lighting director. The lighting director often utilizes different lights, filters, and colors to produce a special effect on the stage.

Lighting directors also work closely with the people handling the light boards and the electricians. A lighting director's job starts at the beginning of rehearsal and ends on opening night, when an electrician takes over running the lights for the actual performances.

Experience in theater is a plus. Lighting designers can earn from $500 to over $150,000 per production.

Makeup Artist

The primary responsibility of a makeup artist is to apply makeup creatively and skillfully to help convey the personality and the look of the characters. A makeup artist can alter the appearance of actors or actresses by making them look older, younger, scarier, or more attractive, depending on the director's character emphasis. Makeup artists in television or film often have to keep an actor from looking washed out due to the bright lights and try to give them a more natural appearance. They work closely with the costume designers and production hairstylists to coordinate the color of makeup with each character's costumes and hair color.

Education and training for this job vary. Some makeup artists have college degrees, some train through internships, and others attend a licensed school of cosmetology and hairstyling. Annual earnings range from $15,000 to $100,000 or more. Some makeup artists earn over $3,000 per week. Those working on major films earn $3,000 per day.

Playwright

A playwright is the person who writes the script for a play or theatrical production. Prior to writing the story, the playwright must develop an idea for the story and then determine how it should be told. Consequently, the playwright may create a script that is a musical, drama, comedy, mystery, or thriller. The play might be an original production or adapted from other sources. In writing this script for the theater, the playwright is responsible for breathing life into his or her characters with crisp and sparkling dialogue, giving the scenes a certain type of ambiance, and introducing conflict and resolution.

There are no exact educational requirements to be a playwright, although many experts feel that college is very helpful. Many colleges offer majors in theater arts or script writing, and they have programs in which students develop and produce plays.

Earnings in this field are difficult to assess because some playwrights barely make any money while others earn millions.

Press Agent, Personal

The main responsibility of personal press agents is to seek as much exposure and press for their clients as possible. Press agents develop and implement publicity campaigns that spotlight their clients to the public and all events in which the clients participate. They work with a variety of entertainers, including actors, performing artists, models, singers, dancers, musicians, comedians, and sports personalities, and book them at entertainment events such as festivals, concerts, theatrical productions, and sporting events. To draw the attention of the media, press agents frequently write and distribute press releases, media kits, articles, biographies, and more. In addition, they may set up press conferences and arrange interviews between the media and their clients.

A bachelor's degree is preferred for this position. A press agent must be creative, have strong written and verbal skills, and have experience working in the entertainment industry. Pay ranges from $20,000 to over $150,000 per year.

Press Agent, Theatrical

The role of a theatrical press agent is to generate as much publicity about a theatrical production as possible in order to generate ticket sales. This person must be aggressive and creative in competing for the attention of the media, which in turn makes the public aware of a particular show. The theatrical press agent's responsibilities include developing publicity campaigns, compiling press kits, writing press releases, preparing biographies of the cast, and arranging interviews and personal appearances for the production's stars. In addition, the press agent notifies critics and reviewers of the show's opening night to make sure they are in attendance, as well as organizes parties and other media events.

Agents must go through a three-year apprenticeship with a member of the Association of Theatrical Press Agents and Managers (ATPAM). This union negotiates the weekly salaries for theatrical press agents, which range from $600 to over $1,600.

Producer

Producers usually work behind the scenes and oversee the production of feature films, television newscasts, sporting events, comedies, dramas, documentaries, reality programs, musicals, and specials. They must weave together all the various aspects of a production from pre- through postproduction. They are actively involved in the process of writing, editing, budgeting, scheduling, planning, casting, scouting out locations, and hiring personnel for specific productions. Depending on the nature of the program, a producer's role may vary from project to project.

Producers must have a great disposition and be able to handle stress, meet deadlines, stay organized, make decisions, and follow their instincts. They also should be willing to travel. Producers are valued for their ability to complete a film on time and within a budget.

A producer's salary is often determined by the budget of the film, the time the project consumes, the producer's status, and whether or not he or she owns the production company or is hired on as a producer. Producers can earn from $17,000 to $200,000 to $1,000,000 or more per production. Some producers put up their own money to produce a film, then earn a percentage of the profit.

Public Relations and Promotional Director (Television)

The public relations and promotional director plays a key role in the development and implementation of a television station's public relations campaign. This person encourages positive media and public attention for the station through promotional efforts. These may be cosponsored by community organizations, businesses, or station affiliates. The duties of a public relations and promotional director are developing special promotions and contests, scheduling station personalities for interviews or public appearances, developing and writing press releases and other material about the station, and conducting research to determine the station's audience and ways to expand it.

A bachelor's degree is preferred. Earnings are usually $20,000 to $85,000 per year.

Scenic Designer (Theater)

The look and essence of a theatrical production is largely defined by the scenic designer. Scenic designers are responsible for creating the stage sets for both main productions and road productions of shows. Stage sets include backdrops, props, furniture, and lighting. Depending on the requirements for the stage show, these sets can involve elaborate or simple designs. An imaginative designer must work hard to transform the stage into something that is not only memorable but visually illustrates to the audience where the scene is taking place. Designers work under the director and must find a way to bring that director's concepts to life when creating the special effects for a set. Earnings range from $500 to $150,000 or more per production.

Screenwriter

The responsibility of a screenwriter is to write and develop scripts for motion pictures, films, and television programs. A film's potential lies in the strength and uniqueness of the story as told by the screenwriter. Screenwriters must know how to move a story forward and be able to incorporate dialogue, narration, stage directions, and more in their scripts. They must also have a strong understanding of character development, conflict, resolution, viewpoint, and setting.

The average Writer's Guild Association member makes about $50,000 per year. According to an April 2001 *Los Angeles Times* article, one-fourth of the working members of the guild make only the minimum, which is $88,614 for an original screenplay, $23,611 for a rewrite, and $11,800 for a polish. Those who write high-budget feature films can earn over $1 million, plus royalties.

Set Designer

A set designer for television or film develops and designs the sets and scenery for a production. He or she will read the script to figure out what physical sets must be designed and then meet with the director and producer to learn what their ideas are. In addition, the set designer will meet with the lighting designers, costume designers, property masters, set dressers, and carpenters in the production company before developing the set. Set designers must conduct research to make sure that each set is appropriate for a specific time period. They have to develop ideas, sketches, miniature models, and floor plans of the sets for the producer's approval. Once the plans have been approved, the set designer is in charge of the set's construction.

A person with a bachelor's degree and experience is preferred. Courses in graphic arts, drafting, drawing, stagecraft, and architecture are recom-mended. Annual earnings range from $18,000 to $95,000 or more.

Sound Editor

Lighting and visuals certainly have a significant impact on the mood of a film, but sound plays an equally important role. The supervising sound editor is responsible for every sound on the final sound track, except for music. The editor must make sure that the sound the audience hears is authentic and distinct enough to stir their emotions. In postproduction the sound editor is one of the major collaborators, along with the director and film editor, who sets the tone and pace of a film.

Sound editors are heavily involved in working with the dialogue the audience hears in a film to make sure it translates properly. This post–production taping of dialogue, or "looping," also entails adding in any background voices and other sounds (such as footsteps) to the film to add to the reality of the story.

Sound effects technology has advanced tremendously over the years, requiring sound editors to always keep track of the industry's newest developments. The minimum pay for a sound editor is over $30 per hour.

Stage Director (Theater)

The stage director is responsible for interpreting a play and making all the decisions that will determine the scope of the production. He or she works with the designers of scenery, lighting, and costumes before and during rehearsals to set the tone and mood of a theatrical production. The director coordinates the work of everyone involved in the play, including selecting the cast. To create the final product the stage director may also collaborate with his or her assistant director, stage manager, and secretaries.

In the very beginning, most directors work unpaid or for a fee in small productions. It is not until they have accumulated a large body of work that directors have the opportunity to be hired full time. Starting pay is usually in the low twenties. Directors working on Broadway productions typically earn $80,000, plus royalties. A few top stage directors have made millions through their work in highly successful Broadway productions.

Stage Manager (Theater)

The person who works most closely in assisting the stage director is the stage manager. A stage manager is usually involved in every phase of a play and its production. He or she calls the cast together for rehearsals, informs the stars when they need to be ready to go on stage, makes arrangements for stand-ins, gives the signal for the house lights to dim, and announces when the production is about to begin. Moreover, the stage manager maintains the master script, which contains all the details of the play, including actors' movements, entrance and exit cues, costume details, lighting, and sound cues.

The stage manager will also keep personal records on all the cast members and backstage crew. Depending on the size of the production, stage managers often have assistants to help them with backstage duties. This affords them the opportunity to stand out front and watch the play so that they can be aware of any revisions that need to be made.

A degree in theater arts or a related field, plus experience, is preferred. The salary varies depending on the size of the production.

Tour Publicist

Tour publicists go on tour with entertainers and execute all of the artists' publicity from the road. They also handle publicity and promotional details prior to the start of the tour. While on the road, the publicist arranges media interviews, press conferences, parties, photography sessions, and personal appearances for the entertainer. He or she also compiles press kits and writes news releases. The tour publicist must be prepared to handle all dilemmas or problems that occur on the road that may lead to adverse publicity for the artist, and to give any problem a positive spin.

A degree in business or a related field is preferred. A publicist may earn from $25,000 to over $100,000 annually.

Unit Publicist

A unit publicist handles the promotion and publicity for television shows and movies. This person's primary goal is to capture the attention of the media and to attract viewers to new programs or films. The unit publicist must develop and then implement an exciting and creative plan to entice people to watch the show. Interviews are often set up with the local, national, and international media. A publicist may travel and accompany the project's stars to various media events. He or she usually provides press releases, film clips, press kits, and whatever else might be needed to further promote the event. A unit publicist also arranges press conferences and screenings for critics or reviewers.

Unit publicists work from assignment to assignment. The ones working in television are usually retained for longer periods of time. A bachelor's degree is preferred for this job. A unit publicist may earn from $25,000 to over $100,000 annually.

Since childhood, Gregory Nava was determined to follow his heart and carve out a career for himself in the film business. He considers filmmaking "the art form of our time."

PART 2

Profiles of Success

· · · · · · · · · · · · · · · **TABLE OF CONTENTS** · · · · · · · · · · · · · ·

Moctesuma Esparza—Producer
(California)   37

Maria Jimenez Henley—Dancer,
Choregrapher (California)   43

Bel Hernandez-Castilla—Entertainment
Journalist, Dancer, Actress (California)   49

Dennis Edward Leoni—Writer, Producer
(Arizona)   55

George Lopez—Comedian (California)   61

Bill Melendez—Animator, Producer
(Arizona, California)   67

Gregory Nava—Filmmaker, Writer, Director
(California)   74

Emanuel Nuñez—Agent (California)   79

Moctesuma Esparza

Producer

The turning point in Moctesuma Esparza's life was when he mustered up his courage and in a booming voice corrected a teacher who had been butchering his name. The teacher, Tom Telly, asked to see him after class. As it turned out, the teacher decided to recruit Moctesuma for his drama and speech class. Esparza says the only thing that kept him interested in high school was drama, theater, speech competitions, and music. "The performing arts were very important to me, it got me through a non-motivating, non-inspiring high school experience."

But he found out very quickly that there were limited prospects for Mexican American actors. At the time there were very few role models of Mexican descent. So he gave up the notion when he went to college at UCLA and declared history as his major.

However, during his college years his sense of outrage grew over the social injustice that existed in the country, particularly for Mexican Americans. This led Esparza to become a committed activist. He was incensed by the lack of opportunities for and lack of educational attainment of Latinos, and by the fact that Latinos were being discouraged from attending college. There was no expectation or demand by instructors or administrators for Latinos to perform well in school or even graduate from high school.

During his high school years, Esparza cofounded Young Chicanos for Community Action, which transformed into the militant group the Brown Berets and the student community outreach organization United Mexican American Students. In 1968 the group orchestrated the Chicano Blowouts, which led to 20,000 Los Angeles high school students walking out of their schools in protest of inferior education. He was part of a group that came to be called the East L.A. 13. The group was indicted by the Los Angeles Grand Jury under the legalistic theory of conspiracy to commit a misdemeanor, disrupting a public school. After several years of court hearings, motions, and appeals, the charges were dismissed, based on the Bill of Rights provisions of freedom of speech and freedom to assemble to petition the government to redress grievances.

Esparza's activism filtered into his university history class. Esparza had a problem with one of the professors in the history department who had written a textbook on California history. Esparza did not refer to this book in the exams, but he cited alternative texts that had a different outlook on California history. The professor did not appreciate Esparza's answers and gave him an incomplete. He told Esparza he had no future in the history department.

Out of self-preservation, Esparza, then in his third year at UCLA, decided to switch to a film program that he had just created at the university. During this time an African American professor in film school, Eliseo Taylor, asked him to participate in a study of the images of minorities in the media. Esparza helped put together a research study for the university. One of the conclusions reached was that the university needed to persuade minorities to be in its film and journalism school. Esparza then wrote a curriculum to create a program called ethno-communications, with no real intention of being a part of the program. When he first transferred to the program he just wanted to get his degree and move on. Taylor convinced him that he could use his abilities as an organizer to produce films.

When Esparza received a bachelor of arts degree from the film/television division of the theater arts department, he decided to become involved in film as a career. Esparza enrolled in UCLA's film school with the idea of utilizing filmmaking as a vehicle for social change. He wanted to create films that would present Latinos in non-stereotypical ways. He also realized he could have more control over the films' content if he were involved with producing it. He received a master of fine arts degree in 1973. His master's thesis, a documentary he wrote and produced called *Cinco Vidas* (*Five Lives*), was aired by NBC and won an Emmy in 1973.

Since then the exceptionally talented television and feature film producer has received over 100 honors, including an Academy Award nomination, an Emmy, a Clio Award, the Cesar Chavez Award, and Cine Golden Eagle Award. Partnered with Robert Katz in Esparza/Katz Productions, Moctesuma Esparza's film credits over the years include *Price of Glory* (2000), starring Jimmy Smits, Jon Seda, Paul Rodriguez, and Ron Perlman; *Introducing Dorothy Dandridge* (1999) with Halle Berry; *The Disappearance of*

Garcia Lorca (1997), starring Andy Garcia, Esai Morales, Edward James Olmos, and Giancarlo Giannini; *Rough Riders,* a four-hour miniseries starring Tom Berenger and Sam Elliott; *Selena* (1997), starring Jennifer Lopez; *Butter* (1998), starring Nia Long, Shemar Moore, and Ernie Hudson; *A Gift of Giving* (1998), starring Diahann Carroll and Tisha Campbell; *Gettysburg* (1995), a four-hour miniseries featuring Tom Berenger, Jeff Daniels, Martin Sheen, and Sam Elliott; *The Cisco Kid* (1994) with Jimmy Smits and Cheech Marin; *Caliente Y Picante* (1990), a one-hour HBO music special featuring Ruben Blades, Linda Ronstadt, Carlos Santana, Tito Puente, and Ciela Cruz; and *The Milagro Beanfield War* (1988), starring Sonia Braga, Ruben Blades, Melanie Griffith, and Julie Carmen.

After graduate school Esparza initially produced documentaries such as the 1982 PBS special *Borderlands* and the1974 PBS children's program *Villa Alegre.* According to *The Los Angeles Times,* Esparza was one of the first Latino producers to find creative ways of financing pictures. His *Ballad of Gregorio Cortez* (1982), starring Edward James Olmos, was funded through PBS's *American Playhouse* and by preselling the television rights to Europe with a theatrical release window. Esparza's resourcefulness over the past 20 years have led to his working his way from a publicly financed documentarian to an independent producer with studio backing. During the 1980s the filmmaker added to his resume *entertainment executive* when he financed and built a cable television company in East Los Angeles—Buenavision Telecommunications—that brought state-of-the-art cable television to that area of town. For over a decade Buenavision has been acknowledged as having the best customer service record, by far, of all the cable companies in Southern California.

Moctesuma Esparza was born on March 12, 1949, to Mexican immigrant parents in East Los Angeles, California. His mother died giving birth to his younger brother, Jesus, and his aunt Tomasa helped to raise the children. Moctesuma rarely saw his father except on his one day off a week. The times they spent together on that day off were the happiest of his childhood. His father would talk to him about history and politics and about the religions of the world. It was during these times that Moctesuma gained the confidence from his father that he could achieve his goals in life through education.

Moctesuma recalls growing up during the '50s and hearing the words *dirty Mexican* and *spic*. He says, at the time, "being called a Mexican was like being slapped in the face."

Esparza spoke only Spanish until he went to kindergarten. He didn't learn how to read English until fourth grade, although he had been taught by his father to read Spanish years earlier. However, by the fifth grade he excelled in school, and from ninth grade on he was president of every club he joined; and he was named class valedictorian. He cites his English teacher, Tom Telly, as being one of the most powerful influences on his education. Moctesuma read voraciously and was so excited about it that he spent hours reading books in the juvenile collection at the local library.

But as a youth, Esparza found he lived as a marginal person between two worlds. He was an A student yet also in a gang. His father instilled in him a sense of patriotism, but society viewed him as a foreigner. He encountered teachers and counselors at school who discouraged him from dreaming about UCLA and suggested that if he wanted to further his education he should go to a junior college instead. Despite these low expectations, Esparza scored in the top two percentile of the SATs and entered UCLA in the spring of 1967.

What Esparza finds most exciting about being involved in the film industry is "the ability to express my creative vision in film, which is a mass-audience art form. It also provides the opportunity to take the things that I care about and are important to me, which are the nature of what it is to be a human—history, how we come to be what we are, what humans are capable of, both positive expression and also negative expression. And finally, to create works of art that can both entertain and influence people."

When asked about the drawbacks of his career, Esparza says that he doesn't find any. But he does see challenges. "The challenge is that this is a very expensive art form. I have to raise millions and millions of dollars in order to make a movie, so it requires that I be able to convince others who have the purse strings to finance the movies that I want to make, and so that's a challenge, not a drawback."

Esparza advises people who want to break into this business to get the maximum education they can, to go to college and take classes in literature, politics, or philosophy. He strongly encourages students to first discover who they are, what they care about, what stories they want to tell, and then get an education in a specific class of filmmaking, either as directors, writers, producers, or performers. He also feels it would be very beneficial to get a graduate degree in the craft so that you have a mastery of the language of the profession. It will give you a greater understanding of filmmaking so that when you enter the field, you will be competitive.

In his career Esparza has tried to make Latin-themed commercial films that have a crossover appeal, as well as films in many other genres and styles, demonstrating his broad interest and capabilities. Thus far he's been fortunate enough to be able to produce movies such as *Gettysburg* and *Rough Riders* in addition to *Selena* and *Price of Glory.* "Even though there is still institutional racism and external barriers, we now have the power to overcome them and achieve our goals."

Eternally optimistic, Moctesuma Esparza is encouraged by the success of such people as Jennifer Lopez, Ricky Martin, Oscar De La Hoya, Christina Aguilera, and others that are being ac-cepted as American pop culture icons. He feels the floodgates are finally opening.

Perseverance, passion, intensity, commitment to quality, and dedication are probably the defining characteristics of Moctesuma Esparza. But his love for his work may be the single reason Esparza has no plans of slowing down his prodigious film efforts. Among the many projects he has in development is *The Cesar Chavez Story.* His latest film is an epic prequel to *Gettysburg* called *Gods and Generals,* about the start of the American Civil War. He continues to give back to his community through public service and volunteerism. He is the honorary mayor of his community and the chairman of a national Latino business leaders group called The New America Alliance, and he sits on the board of directors of a dozen organizations.

"The greatest gift of life is being able to work at what you love. A lot of people think that getting a job is just something that you have to do in order to stay alive. You've got to put in your time and make the money to support yourself and your family. I think that it is very possible to find a profession that you love and that nurtures your life".

Maria Jimenez Henley

Stage Manager, Assistant Director, Choreographer, and Dancer

Maria Jimenez Henley has lived primarily in Los Angeles. In 1974 she and her husband, Don C. Henley, bought a second vacation home in the resort area of Big Bear Lake, California. This enabled them to continue their careers in Los Angeles, she as a dancer on the Leslie Uggams CBS-TV series and Don as personal manager to Pat Boone and Debby Boone. Maria also owned a country store called The Mother Lode and later a sweater design business. By 1983 the former dancer and choreographer, who had worked in over 200 variety shows, films, and stage shows, had reached a point in her life where she could afford the luxury of not working. She and Don decided to move to Big Bear Lake permanently and raise their two sons, Youree and Raphi. But her whole life turned around when her husband died suddenly on the very morning they were to move. "I didn't know what I was going to do with my life," says Maria. "I thought, I've got to raise two boys that are five and eleven, I don't want to dance anymore, I'm tired of my sweater business, and I'm burned out. . . ."

She decided to go ahead and take the boys to Big Bear to live and try to fulfill Don's dream. After that first year, Maria realized that she would have to find work, so in 1984 she sold the house in Big Bear and moved the family back to Los Angeles. It was a difficult transition for her, but fortunately she ran into some good luck along the way.

"An old dance friend who was producing the sitcom *Punky Brewster* said, 'I didn't know you were back in town. Would you come on and choreograph a tap dance number for twelve kids?' I did, and then they asked me to stay on as a stand-in. It didn't pay much money, but I needed the job. I worked as a stand-in for two and a half years. However, even though they had been good to me, I needed a better paying job. I asked my executive producer, David Duclon, who was getting ready to do a new show at Twentieth Century Fox, if he could take me along and put me on as a stage manager. That led to my first job as a stage manager, on a show called *Second Chance,* which later became *Boys Will Be Boys.*"

Since that time Henley has worked in numerous productions, ranging from sitcoms to variety shows that include *All About Us; One World; Viva Vegas; USA High; Wings; Saved by the Bell; Night Court; California Dreams; Evening Shade; Los Beltrans; Good Morning, Miss Bliss; Desi Arnaz Entertainment Awards; Variety Club Telethon; Hispanic Achievement Awards;* and *Jane Fonda Workout.* Henley also serves as cochair of the Latino Committee in the Director's Guild of America (DGA).

Maria was born in Santa Ana, California, where the Jimenez family lived on an orchard ranch. Later the family moved to Temple City, where Maria and her three siblings went to school. Maria says, "My dad put us in the middle of Temple City and there wasn't a Mexican in sight." The only time she remembers seeing other Mexican people was across the tracks on the poor side of town.

Her father was a painter by trade, but as a hobby he was a hunter, fisherman, and builder. "My father could landscape yards and build rooms and houses, and fireplaces," Maria recalls. "So we had this extraordinarily large wonderful house on three acres that everyone loved in our neighborhood.

The best rosebushes in the world and the prettiest grass."

A self-described tomboy, Maria says she was fearless. She was captain of the baseball team, she was bossy, she fought with the boys—she had to be the best, the fastest, and the strongest. "But I never considered myself pretty," Maria confesses. "I grew up with an inferiority complex. The kids used to call me names, and so that made me a fighter. As a child I was out on the playground kicking butt, making sure they knew who I was, but all the while feeling I was less than somebody because my skin was dark."

Maria attended Rosemead High School, where she was a cheerleader and a majorette and participated in numerous other extracurricular activities. A significant turning point happened early in her life when she went to a modern dance class at a dance studio in Hollywood called Eugene Loring's American School of Dance. Seeing the dancers perform and hearing the music sparked something deep inside her. "I told my mother, 'I know what it is I want to do.' And she said, 'What is that, *mija?*' I said, 'I want to be a dancer.' And she asked, 'How do you do that?' And I said, 'I don't know, but I want to be one.'"

Focusing on becoming a dancer, Maria knew the family couldn't afford the full tuition for dance school, so she applied for and was awarded a full scholarship to attend the renowned American School of Dance. She then had a long discussion with one of the high school administrators as to how she could graduate early. She doubled up on her classes, combining her junior and senior year, and attended summer school while she studied and took dance classes at American School.

Maria's first professional break came when the Broadway hit *West Side Story* was going to be made into a film. Eugene Loring, who was very well known and had choreographed for ballet theater—famous ballets like *Billy the Kid*—became her mentor. He made it possible for her to see a casting person. Jerome Robbins had been holding auditions in Israel, London, Australia, New York, and Los Angeles. Maria had three screen tests, and after six months of auditions she got the call. She was one of only two girls picked from Los Angeles. She was 17 years old and ecstatic. This is what she had been working so hard for. There was no stopping her now. But her plans were almost crushed by something beyond her control.

"It was a Friday and my appendix almost burst. My mother had to rush me to the hospital. They called over the weekend and told my mother I had to be in on Monday morning to begin the first day of class and rehearsals at Samuel Goldwyn's studio, otherwise I would have to be replaced. I cried and begged my mother, 'Please tell them I'll be there. I don't care if I have to crawl.' And that's what I did. I went with my stitches."

Fortunately everything worked out and Maria was able to dance in the movie. She worked on the film for a year and recounts that she met people on the set who became some of her oldest and dearest friends. "We are writing a book together. . . . We have gone through death, divorce, childbirth, drugs, everything. . . . All of us have gone through each other's lives."

After *West Side Story,* Maria Jimenez moved to New York and worked with a number of highly regarded dance companies such as Jerome Robbins's Ballets USA and the Joffrey Ballet. She also worked with Matt Mattox and Lee Theodore, who took her under their wing as a choreographer and worked with her on improvisation and jazz. Maria also assisted Lee on new ballets for the Joffrey Ballet Company, and they and Elliot Feld worked as a team during this creative period. At that time, Henley says, her body was like a machine and she was at the peak of her dancing career. She greatly wanted to do a Broadway show but discovered she was the wrong color and the wrong size. "I'm five-foot-three and dark, and they wanted five-foot-seven, white, blondes and redheads."

Jimenez changed gears and started taking acting classes at the Actor's Studio in New York but ran out of money and returned to Los Angeles. There she studied at Leonard Nimoy and Jeff Corey's acting school. During this time she got an offer from an English producer, Jack Good, to do a special with the Beatles as a dancer and to travel with them for a month. After the tour, the same producer hired her to be an assistant choreographer on a new dance show for ABC called *Shindig*. "It was live. We did ten dances per live show, nonstop, and we had everybody from the Supremes to Ray Charles, Tina Turner, the Righteous Brothers, and the Rolling Stones."

Leonard Nimoy had split with his partner and opened his own repertory company. After working on *Shindig*, Jimenez resumed her acting career and did some plays and theater work at Nimoy's company. It was there that she met her future husband, Don Henley. They became very good friends, and Nimoy was an usher at their wedding. It was her late husband who became Nimoy's recording manager just as his career was beginning to take off with *Star Trek*.

Henley regards her first career as her first passion, but she is equally enthusiastic about her second vocation as a stage manager for the Director's Guild. Working as a first stage manager, Henley says she has to run the entire scheduling and the stage. She explains there are three levels to being a stage manager: The third stage manager may come in two days out of the week to handle extras and block them. The second stage manager comes in two to five days a week and helps the first assistant with the actors and helps out in other ways. Henley, who has worked in all the three levels of stage managing, says that the job of the second is physically the hardest job because you are constantly running after the actors and cuing them. The first stage manager never leaves the floor and decides what's going to be shot and in what order. "It's more of a mind-set," explains Henley. "You take care of the stage and everyone answers to you. If something doesn't work right, or if you've scheduled wrong scenes and it's taking too much time, then they come after you. It's like being a foreman."

Henley forewarns people that it is not easy to get a job as a stage manager. It requires that you be a member of the Director's Guild and that you have a number of years of experience in the industry. You also need three letters from different producers and recommendations from other DGA members, a guarantee of employment on a show, and the producer's guarantee that he or she will use you for either six or twelve episodes. Henley tells people that the job pays very well—one year she made over $100,000—and it has afforded her a pension and a bright future, but she had to pay her dues.

Although progress for Latinos in the industry is still moving at a snail's pace, Henley sees the outlook as being better than before. There is more diversity and there are more women working. "The studios may be giving more lip service than action; however, they are getting more pressure than they've ever had. Now you can turn around and see more directors like Gregory Nava, Carlos Avila, Rey Villalobos, Miguel Higuera, Miguel Arteta, Jeff Valdez, Jesus Trevino, etcetera. They are all crossing over and in that respect it is good. But the numbers are not that terrific. For instance, Sylvia Morales has been in this business for years and she's just getting some directing jobs on *Resurrection Blvd.,* but prior to that it was documentaries, short films, and independent cable assignments.

"So it's not moving fast enough considering the number of Hispanics in the world. The industry has been very good to me and yet my heart breaks because I've sat on so many council meetings [with] people who have DGA cards that are not working." Still, Henley encourages young people to get a solid education both academically and through work experience. But above all, she says, "Whatever you do, have a passion for it. Don't do something you don't want to do, because even when you do things you are passionate about, it's still work. And it helps if you enjoy it."

Bel Hernandez-Castillo

Entertainment Publisher, Dancer, and Actress

Bel Hernandez-Castillo has always been concerned about how Latinos have been portrayed in the media. She states that the reason she became so passionate about images is because she has lived it. Growing up in East Los Angeles, she rarely saw any Latinos on television. The reason for the invisibility of Latinos on the screen became even more apparent when Hernandez decided to pursue a career in acting. The majority of roles she and her peers were repeatedly offered were primarily as maids, prostitutes, addicts, and other characters that did not truthfully represent the Latino population. When a great role was finally on the horizon, her frustrations culminated in 1992.

"New Line Cinema announced they were doing a movie on the Mexican artist Frida Kahlo, and they had cast Laura San Giacomo in the role of Frida," says Hernandez. "They said there were no Latino actresses right for the role. A group of actresses got together; we were upset because the audition process was not open to us. I think there were only two Latina actresses that auditioned. As actors we had been fighting this uphill battle as Latinos trying to work in mainstream Hollywood. And so we put together the protest and we had everyone come out, high-profile actors and all. It wasn't against Laura San Giacomo, it was because we had been locked out of the audition process."

This time Hollywood listened and the project was shelved. But Hernandez had seen this before. Latino activist organizations would chastise Hollywood executives for the lack of work in front of and behind the camera, and promises would be made. Two years later the issues would be forgotten, promises broken, and everything would go back to "normal." Hernandez was determined to not let this happen again and to keep the issues in the forefront by creating a newsletter.

The trade publication she cofounded with Loyda Ramos in 1992, *Latin Heat,* started out as a protest newsletter but evolved into a magazine that no longer simply criticizes the entertainment industry. *Latin Heat* highlights the industry members that are creating opportunities for Latinos and covers the achievements of Latino talent in the media. With its focus on

Latinos in television, film, music, and theater, *Latin Heat* has been recognized as the number one source for entertainment industry news. It has served as a resource for readers and major media outlets such as CNN, *The Wall Street Journal, Hispanic Business, Entertainment Weekly, Us Magazine, Hollywood Reporter, Vogue, MovieMaker, and Hispanic Magazine.*

Starting in 1995, *Latin Heat* has copresented the annual Latino Entertainment Industry Conference, which is a two- to three-day conference filled with panel discussions, luncheons, and the Gala Awards, at which the annual Vision Award is given to an individual in the media arts whose work and contributions have helped uplift the image of Latinos. Past award winners include directors Francis Ford Coppola, Gregory Nava, and Alfonso Arau; actress Rita Moreno; and producer Moctesuma Esparza. Moreover, *Latin Heat* recently partnered with On Line Production Services to create The Latin Heat Online Talent Directory, "the first state-of-the-art searchable Internet directory of Latinos in entertainment."

Along with the tremendous success of the magazine, publisher and editor in chief Bel Hernandez-Castillo is considered one of the leading authorities on Latinos in the entertainment industry. She has frequently served as a panelist or consultant, including a panel at the Smithsonian on Latinos in entertainment and coordinating a roundtable discussion for the *Hollywood Reporter* among six high-profile Latinos working in television. She has also appeared on national and international television and radio shows.

Born in Zacatecas, Mexico, as Belarmina Hernandez, Bel has four brothers and one sister. Her father was killed before she was born.

Eventually her mother remarried, and the family moved to East Los Angeles when Bel was six years old. Bel didn't speak any English, but she remembers learning very quickly and speaking with a heavy accent. She attended Roosevelt High School, one of the largest in the area. At Roosevelt they offered all types of dance classes, including modern dance and ballet. Bel wasn't interested in modern dance or ballet because she thought that they were for white people. However, when a folklorico teacher came in she got excited: "I said, 'That's for me because it's Mexican.' So I started doing Mexican folk dance when I was about sixteen or seventeen." She also started taking ballet, jazz, and tap because her instructor required all her company members to be trained in these dance forms.

After graduating from high school Hernandez took a brief interest in modeling and went to modeling school. Nevertheless, she continued to dance and spent time in Mexico studying with Amalia Hernandez, the renowned folklorico group in Mexico City. During her stay in Mexico she found that despite her Mexican nationality she wasn't accepted as a Mexican and endured endless put-downs for her poorly spoken Spanish and was called a *pocha* (an Americanized Mexican). It was then that she decided to become an American citizen.

When she returned to Los Angeles, Hernandez and her friend Miguel Delgado started a dance group, Mexican Dance Theater. They did a lot of shows, traveling across the country and experimenting with a new dance form of combining Mexican folk dance with contemporary dance forms. By then she was also auditioning for roles in various other shows. She recalls how she felt during these auditions: "I used to think to myself, I don't really think I'm going to be as good as the Anglo girls. But when I got there I realized they were no better. . . . In fact, some of

them were really bad. Again, because I never saw a dancer or anyone on screen that was Latina, I figured we must not be good."

Around this time Miguel got a job as a choreographer for Luis Valdez's *Zoot Suit.* When the first cast went to Broadway, they had to recast some of the roles in Los Angeles. Hernandez auditioned for a dance role that required understudying an acting role, and at the time she had no prior acting experience. She recalls how Valdez responded to her scene: "It was so bad when I finished my scene and he started laughing in his loud heavy voice—he thought it was hilarious! But I didn't care," she laughs. "I got into the play and it was great. The play was a historical landmark for Latinos in Los Angeles theater, running over a year. There was a standing ovation every night. There were celebrities and movie stars in the audience, and I thought, Wow, I like acting."

It was during this time that Hernandez met her husband-to-be, Enrique Castillo, who was playing the lead of Henry Reyna in *Zoot Suit.* They have been together for over 20 years and have an 11-year-old daughter, Karina Castillo. After *Zoot Suit* Hernandez continued to pursue acting and appeared in film, television, and theater shows, including *Selena, Scenes From Everyday Life, Colors, Losin' It, Body and Soul, My Family/Mi Familia, Beverly Hills 90210* (pilot), *Crime & Punishment, Saved by the Bell, L.A. Law, Chicago Hope, Laurel Canyon* (pilot), *La Carpa,* and *Drug Wars.*

Hernandez toys with the idea of occasionally acting again because she still receives offers to do film and television. But for now her commitment has been on expanding her trade publication internationally. Her current plans are to reach out to Spain, Brazil, Mexico, and Latin America, because there isn't a trade publication that focuses on the Latino entertainment industry in these countries. "We will be adding a Spanish section for our expansion into Latin American countries," says Hernandez. Ironically, she finds that people already automatically assume the magazine is in Spanish.

"The capital of the entertainment industry is Hollywood," remarks Hernandez. "The vast majority of executives and people who work in these industries don't read Spanish, so why would I want to make it in Spanish? Plus, I want Hollywood to know that there's this vibrant pool of talent that speaks English. And although we cover Spanish-language TV as well, I think this is an area that needs attention.

"Our magazine has brought attention to the fact that not all Latinos speak Spanish and we don't all watch Spanish-language television. Sixty percent of us watch English-language TV and would like to see ourselves reflected on mainstream network television and on the big screen in roles that match what we are—doctors, lawyers, educators, supervisors, professionals. . . . That is reality, not the stereotypes we keep getting. Filmmakers like Miguel Arteta, Gregory Nava, Alfonso Arau, and others have been revolutionizing the Latino image and cultivating it and presenting a different image so that people can see a wider spectrum of Latino life."

Hernandez gives credit to Ricky Martin for decisively blasting the doors loose and making being Latino hip, letting the work other Latino filmmakers and activists had been doing for years break through on a global scale. She finds that many more producers and finance companies are showing an openness to look at Latino projects and cater to this market, especially since it is the number one moviegoing audience.

"I think magazines like *Latin Heat* have played a very important role in creating stars because *Latin Heat* covered Jennifer Lopez when she was still a fly girl," Hernandez comments. "It was our job to hone in on any Latino that came to town. For example, another actor who is up and coming and is really hot now is Jay Hernandez. He is costarring in *Crazy/Beautiful* with Kirsten Dunst. His manager called and thanked us for promoting his talent and the fact that we have given him more coverage than the major magazines.

"And to me, that has been one of the detriments to the U.S. English-speaking Latino actor, the lack of publicity and avenues to publicize what he or she is doing. Actor Pepe Serna has been in the business since he was in his early teens. He has done over three hundred films, but not many people know who he is. I blame that on the lack of avenues for coverage."

Nevertheless, Hernandez sees things changing and feels that Latino talent is finally getting recognition. But she also stresses that in order for it to be consistent, the Latino community has to realize that it is not a matter of entitlement or a given.

"I think it's going to change because we have something valid to tell and we are telling it. But we have to drive our own stories and we have to take charge and get into the green lighting positions [executive-level positions; these executives can say which projects will be done]. No one is going to give us anything. We have to go out and do it and make it profitable.

"Films like *Spy Kids* by Robert Rodriguez are so important because it is a mainstream film. The family is Latino, but they don't beat you over the head with it by having them talk about the barrio or having them eating Mexican food. . . . It's just a fact that they are Latinos and their name happens to be Cortez. I believe that's what the Latino image in Hollywood will evolve into—mainstream. Our magazine, *Latin Heat,* will also evolve into a mainstream publication with our focus still on the fastest-growing segment of the U.S. population, Latinos."

Dennis Edward Leoni

Writer, Producer

Before moving to Los Angeles, while he was in Hawaii, Dennis Leoni wrote his first screenplay. He never sold it, but it attracted enough attention to get him an agent and his first writing assignment. Since that time Leoni has been able to firmly establish himself as a writer and producer in the television and film industry. He is the creator, writer, and executive producer of the popular Showtime series *Resurrection Blvd.* The series focuses on the Santiagos, a family whose hopes and dreams are rooted in the world of professional boxing.

"*Resurrection Blvd.* was inspired by my own family experiences growing up in Tucson, Arizona," remarks Leoni. "It's about real life and real people. Setting the show in the world of boxing gives us a darker, edgier feel than your usual family drama, Latino or otherwise."

The program is also the first dramatic series on television to showcase Latinos prominently both in front of and behind the camera. *Resurrection Blvd.* features a remarkable cast composed of veterans and newcomers. It includes Tony Plana, Michael DeLorenzo, Elizabeth Peña, Nicholas Gonzalez, Ruth Livier, Marisol Nichols, and Mauricio Mendoza.

Dennis Leoni was born and raised in Tucson, Arizona. After he attended the University of Arizona, he began his career in the movie and television business as an actor/stuntman at the famous western movie location Old Tucson. "We would do stunt shows when the movies would come to town," recalls Leoni. "I'd get a little horse riding part, falling off a building, a gunfight, or something." He remained there for two years, later becoming the director of the acting department and appearing in movies, television shows, and commercials. Afterward Leoni moved to Hawaii, where he continued his acting career. Eventually he worked his way into production on the classic television series *Hawaii Five-O.*

Leoni's television and film credits include *Resurrection Blvd., Almost a Woman, Untombed, McKenna, Covington Cross, Raven, Hull Street High, Mystagogue, The Madness of Hanna Louise, The Collingwood Massacre,* and *The Haunted White House.* He has also been honored with awards such as the Alma Award, Golden Eagle, Vision Award, and Impact Award.

Leoni finds that working as a writer and producer is the good thing about being in series television. He explains that the writers become show runners because the shows are there. They have to be done on a weekly basis so the writer takes a prominent role. A writer creates the show and it remains the writer's vision.

"There are lots of exciting things about my job," Leoni says. "Watching something come to life that you went in a room and thought up is always very exciting to me. It amazes me that they pay me money to go sit in a room and make stuff up and the next thing you know we're spending lots of money to make it come to life."

Leoni states that the film business is very tough and competitive. He's met a lot of great people as well as people who have been very disappointing and not very nice. "Whenever there are large sums of money involved in anything, I think ego sort of takes over, and dealing with people's egos is not always an easy thing."

Leoni thinks that although progress may be slow, the entertainment industry is starting to become more accessible to Latinos. "You just have to per-severe in hopes that you will get a chance, and when you get your chance, you're ready to take that chance and run with it!"

To be successful in this field, Leoni emphasizes that you must write well. As a kid he didn't see himself as a good writer. But realizing those limitations, he did his best to improve. "When you find something that you want to do you just have to keep trying and work as hard as you can to learn all the things that you can. There are lots of differ-ent kinds of writing and you just need to find where your strengths are and play to those strengths. Try to find the proper niche for yourself so that you can excel at what you're good at."

Leoni adamantly believes that read-ing is the key ingredient to writing. "You can learn so much by reading," he stresses. "Go to the library and learn anything you want to. Experience things you will never experience in your life. Someone has and you can see it through their eyes. Live vicariously through them and see and experience things that only a few people get to experience. Read about everything, even if you don't think it is applicable. I'm surprised by the things I thought I would never apply in my life that I can now apply. Somewhere along the road you realize that knowledge can come in handy."

Something else that is good for writing, Leoni advises, is to listen to dialogue. He states that when you have an ear for dialogue that rings true, and that is succinct and honest, people will know it's not just somebody making something up. Observation is also important. "You can pick things up from people's mannerisms, quirks, and their characters. And that's how I build my characters. They're usually a composite of all the people that I've met throughout my life."

The film business pays very well, and there are writers who have become very wealthy in this profession. But there are plenty writers who aren't rich but who do make a good living. Leoni likens monetary success in this business to rolling dice. Some people have written scripts on speculation and sold them for a lot of money. Leoni did not sell his first spec script, but he worked his way up and now has his own successful show. According to Leoni, a staff writer will make about $5,000 to $10,000 a week as a starting salary. He tells aspiring writers having excellent writing samples can help you get a good agent. A good agent will put your material out there, and if those samples are judged as good, chances are you can get some kind of job. It may not be the best series or the best show, but it will help you get work, and from there you can prove yourself. But he also warns writers that it's not only their viewpoint that matters.

"It's about being collaborative. There's a whole lot of things that you need to bring to the table when you become a writer and you're working with a multitude of people in a collaborative situation. The writers have to learn to work with directors, producers, editors, and all the ancillary people—the costumers, [advertisers], transportation people, music people, and so on. There are probably 150 to 200 people on *Resurrection Blvd.,* and the important thing is that everybody has to work together."

When Leoni got into television writing, there were no other Latino show runners. He looked to mainstream TV to learn the craft of screen writing, and through that he learned to apply his own voice. He learned the basics of writing and drama in a family and applied that to his own Latino family. That's how he came up with *Resurrection Blvd.*

"My average workday is a twenty-four-hour job while you're in production," remarks Leoni. "What you end up doing is dreaming about the job when you're not there. I am in charge of the stories from the very beginning. Most of the stories from the first season are my ideas, and taking those ideas and building stories out of them. It's called breaking a story and then turning it into a synopsis. From there it goes to an outline and then to a script. From that script we go to multiple rewrites, and then we go into production.

"I'm in charge of production on what we're shooting, [and] preproduction of what we [will be] shooting. I'm in development on the scripts that are three ahead. Then we're in production on one script and postproduction on four scripts. So there's about nine stories that I'm doing at any one time, going from development to editing to the dub to all the way through. I'm juggling nine balls at once.

"I usually get up at five or six in the morning. I'll come to work. I will check all mail. I will look at what's going to be shot that day, look over a call sheet to make sure there are no production problems for that day, and then I will either go to editing or I will go to the story room with the other writers and help them break out the stories. Or I'll go talk to one of the other editors or post people and make sure the editing on the episodes that we're working on is ready to go. I'll check to see that the looping is being done or that the dub is ready. I need to go to the mixing stage so that we mix the final sound. Everything is put in steps and I just have to make sure that every step is done.

"Like the other day, I had editing and then the composer came in and I listened to all the tunes that he had for episode eleven. Then we had a cast read-through of episode seventeen. Afterwards I went to the editing room and edited episode fourteen, and then I had notes on episode thirteen from the network and the studio.

"I get about four or five hours of sleep at night. Sometimes when I get home I have to look at a rough-cut tape so that I'm prepared to go into the editing room the next day, or I'll read a script that is still in development and needs to be rewritten. I might even rewrite a little bit. There's any number of things I can do along the way."

Leoni believes the key to his success breaks down into percentages of talent, luck, hard work, and the ability to persevere and outlast the many people who haven't been able to stay in the game and compete.

"The best advice I can give to anyone is to be prepared. No matter what it is. A good education prepares you for whatever you might need. Be prepared with your writing in case someone makes an offer to read it. But don't expect too much too fast. I think nowadays deferred gratification is a lost virtue. People expect the easy road.

"I've been writing for over twenty years. It hasn't been an easy road. You just have to understand that hard work is a major part of this. There are people who do get lucky and it seems easy for them, but in reality nothing is easy. You pay the price sometimes when you try to take the easy road because when you don't have the skills you can get lost in this very tough business. So you just need to be ready. *Resurrection Blvd.* is the first series in the history of American TV that was written, produced, starring, directed, that is all Latino. I'm very proud of that. I never thought that I would be able to get here, but we have and I am very proud of that."

George Lopez

Comedian

George Lopez, one of the top stand-up comedians in the country, says that he was not the typical class clown in high school. "I was not really that outgoing," he comments. "I mostly joked around with my friends. It was their attention I craved more than the school. In school I was really anonymous. I hung out with the same group of guys, but I was the funniest guy they had ever seen in their lives. The word got out in high school and people used to stand in the doorway of the class I was in because they heard I was very funny. But when they were there, I wouldn't do anything because I saw them looking. When people expected it, I wasn't funny. Which is completely different now, because they expect it every day."

Now a longtime fixture in local comedy clubs and on the road, Lopez is dishing out humor regularly to the listening audience as a morning personality on KCMG-FM 92.3, known as Mega 92.3. The radio station's management has high hopes that Lopez will help solidify and build on the pop and R & B station's following in the English-speaking Latino community.

Mega's program director, Mike Marino, told *The Los Angeles Times* that the move is pretty dramatic because "George will be the only Latino celebrity on radio in the number one market in the country speaking English." The gamble is paying off. Already Lopez's presence has boosted the show's ratings significantly.

Lopez states that the Mega show is a perfect fit for him because it has been geared toward a Latino audience. "I've appeared on enough of their shows to know that the people who come to see me are the people who listen to Mega."

It was Roy Laughlin, vice president and general manager of Mega, KYSR-FM Star 98.7, and KIIS-FM that heard Lopez on Rick Dees' show and told him that something could happen for him on radio in Los Angeles. In fact, he saw Lopez as not only increasing the Latino audience, but also establishing a broad coalition of listeners. When his company bought Mega 92.3, he immediately called Lopez and asked him if he'd like to do the show.

"I told him I had no reservations about doing the show because I thought Los Angeles was ripe to be taken over by a Chicano person who wasn't a politician with an agenda or by an actor. Comedy has always been the thread that connects people together. And I do it by talking about all those things, news and culture. And I don't divide, I include. If you can be a Mexican American comedian and draw white, black, Asian, and Latino people, then you are doing something that no other Chicano has ever been able to do other than Cesar Chavez, and though he was absolutely brilliant, he wasn't the funniest brother in the bunch."

Born in 1961 at General Hospital in Los Angeles, George Lopez is an only child. He was raised in the San Fernando Valley by his grandparents, who were older and very strict. He says they were good with the structure of life, but not very nurturing.

"What I try to tell kids now is to nurture yourself and your friends and family if you don't get it from them. You see a bunch of little Latino kids who aren't raised very emotional because the family isn't so. I was at this birthday party and the kids looked tranquilized. They didn't know how to show joy, and I think that's really cultural. We raised our daughter to be outgoing, and when they brought out the cake she was jumping up and down.

One of the parents said, 'Look how happy she is.' I couldn't believe it. They were actually surprised that a kid could be excited about a cake coming out. My wife said, 'It's a birthday cake, what kid isn't happy with a cake?'

"It's control through suppression. It's like if they say, 'You kids go play over there, but you play quietly.' Now what kid do you know can play quietly? I think it's all suppression. It breeds passiveness and I think that's one of the things holding us back. So I tell kids to jump for joy, get crazy, excited, run, and have fun.

"I was tortured as a kid. I craved attention. I tried to get it at school because I wasn't getting it at home. And I think it was at the expense of a quality education. Thank God, I turned all the time I spent [acting out] into an actual career."

School was tough for Lopez. He barely graduated high school and suspects he had a learning disability that went undetected. It hindered his reading and comprehension ability. "Everything I did was auditory," says Lopez. "I can remember things immediately, but if you asked me to sit down and read something, I couldn't tell you. But if you told me about the page, I'd remember forever. My other senses are much keener than my actual [reading] comprehension skills.

"I share this with kids because sometimes if you're doing bad in school, everyone wants to put a label on you. A lot of times it goes undetected and teachers and family think you're just being lazy if you don't understand. If you have a learning disability, they can force you to sit and read all day and it won't make a difference. I advise students that if they are having problems, talk to a counselor and administrator and ask questions. I never did. If I had I probably could have gotten this information twenty-five years ago."

As a child, Lopez dreamed about being a comedian. He was a huge fan of Cheech and Chong and gravitated toward doing stand-up. But when he saw the late comedian Freddie Prinze for the first time, he was blown away. "It was like love at first sight," remarks Lopez. "I was never the same."

Ironically, Lopez's current manager, Ron DeBlasio, was formerly the manager for Freddie Prinze. The two were very close. When Freddie Prinze committed suicide, DeBlasio was devastated. He decided to leave the stand-up business. Lopez was stunned when DeBlasio approached him about becoming his manager.

"He saw me open for Vikki Carr a year ago at the Cerritos Center for the Performing Arts," remembers Lopez. "I recognized his name because I had studied Freddie Prinze. When I met Ron, I thought, 'Wow. . . . That's Freddie's guy,' and now he and I are together. We may not be as tight as he and Freddie were, but we're definitely close. It's an amazing story because here's a guy I idolized and now his manager's my manager."

Since he was 18 years old, Lopez dabbled with being a professional comic, appearing at clubs here and there. But he didn't truly respect it until he was in his mid-20s. At that time a friend told him that he was a "quitter," a "wannabe comedian."

"I thought, wow, if my best friend is telling me this, then I must really be a quitter. I wasn't self-motivating and I wasn't comfortable on stage. I had every strike against me a comedian could have—I wasn't prepared, I wasn't confident, and I was scared to death. But I fought through all that because I wanted it more than the fear. Everybody is afraid of things to try in life, but when you want it more than the fear, your will overcomes it."

Even though Lopez was determined to become a successful stand-up comedian, it wasn't easy. He remembers going to every club he could—The Comedy Store, The Improv—and waiting in line for his opportunity to perform on amateur night. He also remembers quitting several times and driving home on the freeway, thinking, Man, this is impossible. But he'd sleep it off and wake up the next morning and start all over again.

"One time I was so afraid, I put my name in the hat under a different name. Well, this guy pulls the name out of the hat and says, 'E. A. Arland.' And I said, 'Oh my God, that's me!' So I went on stage as E. A. Arland, and that's how anonymous I was, because no one said, 'That's not E. A. Arland—that's George Lopez.' But as I was leaving after my performance the guy said, 'Great job, E.A.' It was the only time I worked under another name."

Lopez remembers two significant turning points in his early career. The first was in 1987. He was working in Las Vegas in the Playboy Girls of Rock and Roll. At a party later that evening he met Richard Correll, who was directing a new movie called *Ski Patrol.* They had a great conversation and Correll decided he wanted Lopez in his movie. Lopez, who had never seen a script before, didn't even have to audition for the part. The movie made money, Lopez got his SAG (Screen Actors Guild) card, and he has maintained it for 12 years. The other significant moment was when he met Arsenio Hall in 1989. Hall was so impressed with Lopez that Lopez appeared on his talk show 15 times during its run.

Lopez continued to do only stand-up comedy because he found it easier than accepting stereotypical acting roles. "The acting parts that were sent to me were drug dealer–type roles. I turned all of them down, even now, because it's more important to me to be proud of myself than it is to portray dealers and criminals. A lot of people thought I was crazy to turn down parts. They'd say, 'Go ahead and do it, you're only acting.' But I couldn't do it.

"I had a huge fight with these actors one time because they said, 'We're all role models.' And I said, 'I don't think you guys are role models. You all play maids, pimps, dealers, and killers in movies.' They said, 'Well, we're acting.' I told them, 'Acting is an image you put out there for kids to see.' I was trying to tell them that if you don't put [a good image] out there, then people can't see it."

Lopez has been doing comedy for so long it's like second nature. He finds he can polish and refine his act in his head. When he performs in a club, he likens it to jazz improvisation: "Whatever comes to my heart is what I say." Although with TV it's more structured, but even then he's been known to ad lib. One of the highlights of his career was obtaining one of the last five spots on *The Tonight Show Starring Johnny Carson*.

"It was like winning the golden ticket. I was one of the last comedians to get on. And I was really afraid. When you hear that theme song and you know what it's for and you know it's real . . . man, I walked out of the curtain and I looked at him and it was like an out-of-body experience."

Although Lopez has been putting in long hours on his radio show and is not currently on the road, he continues to do stand-up comedy in the Los Angeles area. He has also completed work on the Showtime miniseries *Fidel;* a feature film called *Bread and Roses,* which premiered at the Cannes Film Festival; and a couple of episodes of *Resurrection Blvd.*

The advice Lopez offers to new comedians is this: "Go with your basic comedic instincts. Be yourself, and whatever makes you laugh is what you want to convey to the audience, not the opposite or what you think the audience is going to laugh at. Find the things that make you laugh, and if you can't find any then keep working on it till you do. And finally, dream as hard as you can and for everything you can. The worst thing that could happen is it might come true."

Bill Melendez

Animator, Producer

Not many people have lived a fairy-tale life, but Bill Melendez has gotten about as close to it as you can get. With a personality as engaging as his animations, Bill Melendez is one of the world's most successful and highly esteemed animators. He has worked non-stop in film production since he was hired by Walt Disney, where he worked as an assistant animator on such films as *Fantasia, Pinocchio, Bambi, The Wind in the Willows, Dumbo,* and many of the Mickey Mouse and Donald Duck cartoons.

However, Melendez, along with his business partner, Lee Mendelson, is primarily known for bringing the *Peanuts* gang to life in animated versions of Charles M. Schulz's cartoon. Melendez enjoyed a close association with the late Charles Schulz for 44 years. Together they created a library of *Peanuts* programming, including 63 half-hour specials, 5 one-hour specials, 4 feature films, and 372 commercials.

The 84-year-old animator, who speaks with enough enthusiasm to be headed for another 84 years, has been bestowed with hundreds of awards and honors, including eight Emmys and the prestigious George Peabody Award.

Born in Hermosillo, Sonora, Mexico, in 1916, José Cuanhtemoc (Bill) Melendez was raised among a family of ranchers. "As a kid I used to walk around with a big tall glass, and whenever I was thirsty, I'd point to someone and they'd take me to my cow and squeeze me out a glass of milk. It was the best-tasting milk ever," he recalls fondly.

Bill Melendez, his two brothers, and a sister grew up with their mother and her side of the family. Bill saw his father sporadically, but he was not around much. He was a military man and was often away in the service. When Bill was around 10 years old, his mother decided to move the family to the small town of Douglas, Arizona, to give the kids the opportunity to learn English and to seek a better life. They remained in Douglas for about two years before moving to Los Angeles, where they had a lot of relatives and where more and better opportunities existed. Bill remembers seeing bean fields, orange groves, and people driving Model Ts before the family settled in Los Angeles.

At a very early age, Melendez remembers, he was drawing all the time—horses, cattle, and cowboys. At the time he had raw talent but no formal training. After graduating from high school, he planned on attending college because he wanted to become an engineer. However, it was during the heart of the Great Depression and his mother told him he would have to go out and get a job. During this time a friend told him that a guy named Walt Disney was hiring artists in Hollywood. Melendez had no idea who Disney was, but he knew he could draw, so he headed over to the studio to apply for a job.

"And that's when I found out I couldn't draw," Melendez laughs. "They told me, 'You have talent, but you don't have any training at all.' But they said, 'We'll hire you anyway.'" It was the luckiest thing that ever happened to Melendez because it led to a long and enriching career. Melendez would work at Disney for eight hours a day and then attend classes at night to learn how to draw. He also learned that animation wasn't all about drawing designs in a cartoon fashion, but

drawing as close to live action as possible.

"I fell in love with animation right then and there," says Melendez. "It was pretty exciting because those guys were making a living doing this. At the time they were finishing *Snow White*. They were starting to work on another film called *Pinocchio,* which they put me to work on. I didn't know what I was doing, but I was so happy to be trained and get paid for it I couldn't believe it. I assisted whoever needed help. It was really a great adventure, and now I have been working in animation for sixty-four years."

After about four years, Melendez left Disney and worked for Leon Schlesinger Cartoons, which later became Warner Bros. Cartoons. Before he started working at Warner Bros., he was told that unlike Disney, it was a dirty raunchy studio. "It was!" says Melendez. "And I loved it. It was full of drawings on the wall and just a mess. But I met a bunch of wonderful guys who helped me along. My director was Bob Clampett. It was a joy working with that guy and a great experience. He was crazy! And he was a real cartoonist. And that's what I liked.

"Working at Warner's was different in attitude and everything than Disney.

It was more cartoony. At Disney I gained an appreciation of art and went to galleries and museums. It opened my eyes as a young artist. At Warner's they didn't care about drawing, they cartooned. It was another attitude that was very fitting for an animator."

At Warner Bros., Melendez met the late Mel Blanc, known as the man of a thousand voices, who was the voice of many of the most popular and beloved Warner Bros. cartoon characters such as Bugs Bunny, Woody Woodpecker, Daffy Duck, Porky Pig, Tweety Pie, Sylvester, and many others: "Mel was a good friend of mine. He was one of the great decent people that I had ever met in this business, completely unselfish. Usually voice people are very jealous of their jobs, but not Mel. He'd share the bounty. He was a wonderful guy."

After about three years Melendez left to serve in the army for a year, then he returned to Warner Bros. In 1948 he left Warners' to work for United Productions of America (UPA). His projects there included such noted shorts as *Madeline, Gerald McBoing-Boing,* and numerous television commercials. "UPA was an innovative studio where they were doing the most innovative animation of all. They were experimenting with stylized cartoon animation and I had the opportunity to be there."

Thereafter, Melendez decided to work for a maverick producer, John Sutherland, whom he had met at Disney and who had started a very successful studio. Melendez spent the next 10 years directing industrial films for John Sutherland Productions and producing and directing over one thousand TV spots for Playhouse Pictures. He says, "It was another great training experience because I started directing and doing films that were completely different. Not just storytelling films, but educational films. And I discovered that this was a great medium."

The medium rewarded him well, because during this time Melendez won international acclaim at the Cannes, Edinburgh, and Venice Film Festivals in addition to over 150 advertising awards. He also won three Art Director's Medals between 1957 and 1961.

Afterward, Melendez decided to form his own company making television commercials. He started doing work for the J. Walter Thompson Ad Agency, which at the time was the largest advertising agency in the world and whose clients included Ford Motor

Company. The car manufacturer was looking to use animated characters to sell their cars on television and had convinced Charles Schulz to use his cartoon characters from *Peanuts*. Melendez was given the chance to audition with the creator of the script and took his portfolio containing samples and commercials to Schulz's home in Sebastopol, near San Francisco.

"The reason I got to meet him is because he didn't want any Hollywood or New York types messing with his strip. He didn't trust them. And I thought, there's a man after my own heart. So I met Schulz and we hit it off. He liked my work and said, 'Let's try one,' and the rest is history."

That history started out with the two of them doing commercials. Around this time, Melendez hooked up with Lee Mendelson, who was making a documentary called *A Day in the Life of Charles Schulz*. Lee became his partner and executive producer. They were offered the opportunity to do a one-hour Christmas show featuring the *Peanuts* characters four months before Christmas. Melendez told them there was no way he could do a show like that in less than a year. "I said a half hour, no longer," recalls Melendez.

"They took my word like I was a philosopher of the business."

In 1964 Bill produced his first television special, *A Charlie Brown Christmas,* despite being forced to bring it in on a short schedule and tight budget. The program was a major hit.

"When we first finished it I thought at first we killed it and that it was a terrible job. But it wasn't. It had a unique feature in it and captured the heart of this country. I remember when Schulz first told me that Linus was going to give a dissertation from the Bible about the true meaning of Christmas, I said to him, 'Sparky (everyone called him that), this is religious, we shouldn't do this.' And he looked at me with those German blue eyes and said, 'Bill, if we don't do it, who will?' And I told him, 'You've got a point, let's do it!'"

From there other programs followed, including *Charlie Brown's All-Stars; It's the Great Pumpkin, Charlie Brown;* and four feature-length motion pictures—*A Boy Named Charlie Brown* (nominated for an Oscar); *Snoopy Come Home; Race for Your Life, Charlie Brown;* and *Bon Voyage, Charlie Brown.*

Melendez describes the process he and Schulz went through while working on a project: "Schulz would have an idea in his head and we'd sit down and start talking about it. I'd put down notes on my storyboard or I'd tape his conversation. After the meeting I'd come back to my studio and start doing a storyboard. I found out after constantly working on these projects that I needed precisely 360 drawings to make a half-hour show. If I had more than 360 drawings, then we would discuss where to edit."

The close relationship between Melendez and Schulz resulted in a special and fruitful offering of work. But Melendez stresses that the most important thing about their association is that Melendez assured Schulz, "I'm not going to change your designs, Sparky, or anything about your dreams." Just before Charles Schulz died he told Bill, "You're an animator and you can't do my comic strips, but neither can I animate what you do. As long as you do your thing and I do my thing we're going to be successful.' And I thought, after all these years, what a wonderful sensitive person."

Melendez has continued to carry on the legacy of his friend. In addition to commercials, he is working on some of Schulz's uncompleted *Peanuts* projects. "I will never allow anyone to change Sparky's drawings," Melendez vows. "We're going to do it the same way we always have, flat drawings, but we'll create the illusion of animation."

In 1970 Melendez opened a studio in London that produces commercials and other projects for international television. Other work by Melendez includes specials based on the *Babar the Elephant* books; *Dick Deadeye* (based on the work of Gilbert and Sullivan); *Yes, Virginia, There Is a Santa Claus; The Lion, the Witch and the Wardrobe* (based on C.S. Lewis' *Chronicles of Narnia*); and the comic strips *Garfield the Cat* and *Cathy*.

The advice Melendez gives to aspiring animators is this: "All animation is the illustration with drawings of action. If you illustrate somebody crying, then you must draw enough drawings to illustrate somebody crying and then put it on the exposure sheets, shoot it, and if you did it right, it's going to give the illusion that he or she is crying. It's very simple, but you've got to keep it within the framework of the design. Don't change the design, because the reason we get a design from somebody is because it's a very good one and there's a reason for wanting to make it come alive. A drawing is a drawing and just as important as anything. You've got to maintain that integrity. Our job is to respect the work."

Gregory Nava

Filmmaker

"I've loved films and always wanted to make movies since I was a little boy. I used to go see those big epic movies with the parting of the Red Sea and chariot races. I dreamed about being the guy that did that and made it all happen. . . . As a kid I was a great storyteller. I guess if you want to tell stories, that's the thing that immediately attracts you to filmmaking, because that's the art form of our time."

Gregory Nava's passion for storytelling has translated into films that come from the heart—movies that examine such harsh realities as social injustice but also underscore the traditions and heartwarming values of family. The films of this writer and director convey that people are people and that it doesn't make any sense for people who are of a different skin color or who speak a different language to be so often stripped of their humanity. Nava's philosophy is simply this: "I see filmmaking as a tool to bring down the walls that exist between people."

The success of Gregory Nava's films have led to his signing a first-of-its-kind studio deal with New Line Cinema for his newly founded company El Norte Productions to produce and direct Latino-themed movies. New Line Cinema is considered to be one of the first U.S. studios to target Latino audiences. Already El Norte Productions has a slate of films in development, including *Bordertown,* starring Jennifer Lopez as a reporter investigating the murders of young women along the Juarez–El Paso border. Nava is also writing for Jennifer Lopez an adaptation of Victor E. Villaseñor's generational novel *Rain of Gold* and a picture about a baseball team from Monterey, Mexico. Moreover, under the umbrella of El Norte Productions, Nava served as writer, director, and executive producer for the one-hour family drama *American Family,* which was shot in East Los Angeles. The television pilot cast well-known Latino actors such as Edward James Olmos, Constance Marie, Esai Morales, Rachel Welch, and Sonia Braga. The program now has an unprecedented 13-episode deal with PBS. The pilot is scheduled to air in October 2001.

Nava's filmmaking talents first captured Hollywood's attention in 1984 with his classic film *El Norte.* Nava collaborated with his wife, Anna Thomas, and was nominated for an Academy Award for Best Original Screenplay. This moving film explores the lives of a young brother and sister from Guatemala who enter the United States illegally to work. It garnered many international awards. In 1996 *El Norte* was named an American Classic and was designated for special preservation by the Library of Congress. It was one of only 150 American films to be so honored.

Nava directed the feature film *A Time of Destiny,* starring William Hurt and Timothy Hutton, in 1987. In 1995 he cowrote and directed the multigenerational saga *My Family/Mi Familia,* starring Jimmy Smits, Edward James Olmos, Jennifer Lopez, Constance Marie, and Jacob Vargas. The film premiered at the Sundance Film Festival and went on to become a critical and financial success. It was also nominated for an Academy Award. Nava followed this effort in 1997 by writing and directing *Selena,* a movie based on the true story of the slain Tejano music singer Selena, who was on the verge of an English-language crossover when she was killed at the age of 23. The film stars Jennifer Lopez, Edward James Olmos, and Jon Seda. Nava's 1998 film

Why Do Fools Fall in Love was another musical biography, this one based on the life of Frankie Lymon, who was the lead singer for the 1950s rock-and-roll sensation The Teenagers. The movie's stars include Larenz Tate, Vivica Fox, Halle Berry, and Lela Rochon. In 1999 Nava made a documentary for Showtime Network's *In the 20th Century* entitled *American Tapestry,* which takes a look at the past through the eyes of some of Hollywood's most noted directors.

Nava made his first dramatic film while he was attending film school at the University of California, Los Angeles (UCLA). This half-hour film, called *The Journal of Diego Rodriguez Silva,* is based on the life of Garcia Lorca. It earned Nava the Best Dramatic Film Award at the National Student Film Festival. In 1976 his first feature, *The Confessions of Amans,* won the Best First Feature Award at the Chicago International Film Festival.

"I come from a border family," states Nava, who was born and raised in San Diego, California. Many of his Mexicano cousins and uncles lived in Tijuana, so the family constantly drove back and forth across the border, visiting relatives. Nava's father worked at an aircraft plant in San Diego, and his mother was a housewife.

Nava credits his father for being a great influence on his life. "One of the things he told me is that if you are a Mexican American in this society you have to be better. It's not good enough for you to be as good as anyone else— you have to be better. Otherwise you are not going to make it. And I think that was a very beautiful thing. No matter what you think, it's a beautiful country. Yes, there is a tremendous amount of injustice in this country, but we also know there is a tremendous amount of opportunity. I'm making movies in Hollywood and I'm a film director. I've realized my dream and that's a very tough thing to do. So even though it's hard for us, I think that if you work hard you can overcome the obstacles that are placed in front of you. My father was a great role model for me. I saw him have to do that in [his] life and it taught me to do so in mine."

Another person Nava cites as a strong role model was the Mexican painter Frieda Kahlo. He says, "I love people who follow their dreams and overcome the obstacles." Film directors that Nava admires, he says, are "Louis Buñuel, obviously for Latinos, he is so very important. I love Orson Welles' work, I think he's very great. I love Ozu, a Japanese director who did many beautiful films about Japanese family life. They are gorgeous and I have been profoundly influenced by him."

But it is not only artists who have influenced Gregory Nava: he says he has also been inspired by the great leaders who had a social conscience such as Cesar Chavez, Martin Luther King Jr., and Dolores Huerta. "The phrase made famous by Cesar Chavez, *Si Se Puede* ("Yes we can"), is a message that obviously rings throughout everything I've been saying for all Chicanos and everybody who suffers injustice."

The other philosophy that guides Nava's thinking is a very wonderful concept in pre-Columbian thinking known as the Ollin. "It means you find God in the work you do," he explains. "And what you do is very important. Don't be negative, don't be a defeatist. Every single thing that is accomplished is accomplished out of a positive place. We come from a beautiful culture and it is a great ancient culture with wonderful values. We need to embrace ourselves and follow our hearts and dreams. We need to find our Ollin, and when we do that, the whole community becomes stronger."

One of the things that troubles Nava is that there is a tremendous amount of self-hatred that is bred by many things in this society, including the movies and television programs. He says, "The images don't show Latinos in a positive light, and we're taught to not think well of ourselves. So one of the big struggles that we have to learn is to love ourselves and to love who we are. We are all trailblazers and pathfinders. In the film business it feels like this because there aren't a lot of us who [are given the opportunity to] work . . . but it is our right to be a part of this industry to fight for that particular place."

Gregory Nava was determined to follow his heart and dreams and carve out a career for himself in the film business. He remembers making little movies as a child with his parents' movie camera. When he went away to college, he decided to go to the UCLA film school. He states that he was not one of those students who wasn't sure what he wanted to do in school. He focused on filmmaking and film production. He obtained a bachelor's and a master of fine arts in filmmaking, and then he did everything he could to pursue a career as a writer/director in the film industry.

According to Nava, being a film director is one of the toughest jobs there is because you are always in the hot seat. The key to being successful as a director is to be able to communicate with lots of different people. You have to have a vision and then be able to communicate it with the studio executives who are going to give you money, technicians, gaffers, grips, lighting operators, set designers, actors, the press, and so forth. In addition, Nava stresses, being a director requires a great amount of patience and endurance. It's also a very physical job that requires you to be not only physically fit but also strong willed.

"A lot of people aren't going to understand. You might be the only one that sees [your vision]. And sometimes you may have to be a warrior and fight very hard to get your vision up on the screen. Other times you have to be patient, understanding, and compassionate. A filmmaker has to be a very sensitive person because that's what allows you to achieve the beautiful emotions you see on the screen. Plus, you have to be quick on your feet because you may have planned for one thing and another thing happens and your plan goes out the window. Now you're forced to come up with something on the spot."

Nava considers one of the best features in the business is the fact that there are no typical days in his work life. He says, "If I'm writing, I'm alone. I get up when I want, I take breaks when I want. I may stay up and write all night. If we're shooting a movie, I've got to be on the set at five-thirty A.M. I have to direct a labor of hundreds of people. Every day is different. You're in interior, you're in exterior. . . . You're fighting the sun, you haven't got your shot or your lighting.

"When you are in postproduction you have more regular hours. Then you're in with the editor working. When you're not in production or not writing you could be taking meetings all day long or [be] on the phone. That's one of the beautiful things about the film business. It's not the same drudgery every day and there are a lot of different aspects to it."

Working in the film industry can be very tough. Nava states that when he starts working on a film, the length of time it takes to complete the film will vary depending on what is involved in the process. From the beginning of principal photography to actual release is about a year to a year and a half. But it may take years to develop a script that people like. "If you're with a studio, it's easy to get the money if they like your piece," Nava remarks. "If you're trying to finance the movie independently, it could take years. For example, a film like *Mi Familia* took six years to make. It was very hard."

Gregory Nava has one final piece of advice for aspiring filmmakers: "The film business is a very volatile business and it goes up and down. I think you have to have a tremendous amount of self-confidence and belief in yourself and your talents. People who are successful in filmmaking are very passionate about what they want to do and what they want to say. They have something they are burning with. If you're the kind of person that has a dream, that has something so powerful that you have got to get it out and you'll go nuts if you can't say this, then you have the fire and the spirit that it takes to be a filmmaker."

Emanuel Nuñez

Agent

Emanuel Nuñez remembers that when his family immigrated to Miami from Cuba in 1962, it was not the best time to be Cuban in the good old U.S.A. As a kid he grew up with a lot of racism around him, directed at him and his family. It ranged from people saying they refused to rent an apartment to "spics" to slamming the door in their faces. "I remember getting into a lot of fights with kids because of my last name and them not liking my skin color," states Nuñez. "At twenty years old I started not thinking about that stuff anymore, and then twenty-two years later I can't remember much of it."

Much of that may be because Emanuel Nuñez doesn't have time to waste on negative thought. In fact, he doesn't have much time for anything outside of family and career. He's too busy. As one of the top Hollywood agents, Nuñez spends most of his time generating business for his clients, whether it's on the phone, in a conference, or on the road.

Nuñez is certainly not oblivious to Hollywood's reluctance to cast Latinos in more roles, he just refuses to be victimized by the ethnic issue. Working behind the scenes in this industry, Nuñez has made it his goal to create more opportunities for other Latinos. "What I'd like to do is be the person who can open doors or at least set a trail for others and have people follow what I have done. I agree things could be better in terms of Latino and minority hiring. There's always room for improvement. But I think there's a lot of opportunity there and I think it's better to spend the time and energy honestly trying to work and get into these jobs of influence."

He is definitely in a position to do so. As a professional working in the entertainment business for over 20 years, Nuñez works in a beautiful modern office at Creative Artists Agency (CAA) in Beverly Hills, California. His clients are some of the most recognizable names in the business, including Robert De Niro, Al Pacino, Neve Campbell, Gloria Estefan, Antonio Banderas, Glenn Close, Penelope Cruz, Michael Mann, and Ridley Scott.

An only child, Emanuel Nuñez was born on October 23, 1958, in Manzanillo, Cuba, which is on the southern tip of the island. He describes his mother as a "traditional" Latin mother; his father was a CPA in Cuba. Nuñez recalls that the family was in the shoe business. "My grandfather owned a large shoe factory, manufacturing children's shoes, and my father ran the business for him. When Castro took over, everything was nationalized and government-controlled. So when we arrived here, for the first couple of years my father did any kind of work he could get while he learned to speak English."

Despite experiencing racism in his early years, Nuñez says that he had a very good childhood and had a great experience growing up at home with his family and extended family. He didn't always fight back with his fist. Dealing with negativity also motivated him to succeed. He got top grades from elementary school through college. He also was an excellent basketball player and was offered college scholarships. He ended up at Rutgers University in New Jersey and played basketball there for the first semester. However, after a while he realized he wasn't going to be a professional basketball player and started concentrating on his studies, switching his major from medicine to journalism. He earned a degree in jour-nalism with a minor in science. There-after, he moved back to Miami and at-tended Florida International Univer-sity, studying international politics, for two years.

While in school he worked as a news writer at a television station in Miami. It was a small station with a three-man crew. Nuñez worked as a soundman, but he also wrote stories for the re-porter. His goal at the time was to be a journalist, and he loved working in tele-vision.

Nuñez was offered another job as an assistant director at a competing sta-tion, which would have led to his be-ing a director of the weekend news. He didn't take the job because he had a part-time job working for Eastern Air-lines that offered great flying benefits.

During this time, Nuñez took an interest in acting and started taking theater classes. He worked as an actor for about a year, doing commercials and small parts in movies. However, Nuñez's father felt that he was too scat-tered working so many different jobs and offered him a deal in which he'd pay for Nuñez's education and hous-ing and give him a stipend. Nuñez agreed to go back to school, and after being accepted to several law schools chose Pepperdine University in Malibu.

After leaving Pepperdine and passing the bar, Nuñez sought work as an entertainment law attorney. He aggressively applied for work everywhere he could think of, making phone calls and dropping his resume off at studios, production companies, agencies, and large and small firms. He finally got a job working with Art Leeds, an entertainment litigator. Leeds ran a small law firm, but his real interest was entertainment, and he was involved in producing movie and transactional deals, which piqued Nuñez's interest.

Initially Nuñez wanted to practice entertainment law. He felt that if he learned as much as he could from Leeds about entertainment law, eventually he could get a job with a larger firm. However, he soon found out that attorneys handled issues other than pure legal transactions. Nuñez had always assumed entertainment lawyers only reviewed contracts, so that if an entertainment client had real estate issues or a lawsuit the attorney would handle it.

"I didn't really understand the transactional side of it, meaning if they were involved in making a deal, someone would say, I want to buy this book, they want to hire me, what do you think I should get for it? I learned that a lot of that type of work fell under the heading of business affairs. I decided that instead of being an entertainment lawyer, I'd rather be a business affairs executive at a studio, production company, network, or agency."

Through a man who was a senior agent at International Creative Management (ICM), Nuñez was introduced to the head of business affairs for ICM. Nuñez offered to work for free and pursued a position at the company for six months. Eventually he was hired as a junior business affairs person, and after six months he was promoted into a business affairs position.

Soon Nuñez was offered an opportunity to work in the new international division, primarily because he spoke Spanish. He accepted the position and worked as an assistant for a year and a half before he was promoted to full agent. He stayed at ICM for about two years until he was offered a job at CAA, which is the company he really wanted to work for. He considered CAA the leaders in the field. Before he was offered the job, he went through a massive interview process during which he was interviewed by 11 agents. In April 1991 he began working at CAA, and he has been there ever since.

A typical workday for Nuñez entails a tremendous amount of phone calls and meetings. He says that when he first started working at CAA he was told to sit back and let the process happen. He tried it and it made him nuts.

"Your responsibility is to manage and oversee a client's career. And to do so, you have to have an entrepreneurial attitude. When I go to my office on Monday, no one tells me what to do. I know what to do and it's been that way for ten years. The first thing you do when you become an agent is to think, 'Oh boy, I'm an agent, this is great,' and you sit down at the phone and you think something is going to happen. If you wait for something to happen, you're not in the right business.

"You can either sit in your office and wait for someone to call, or you can get up and go to an agent next door and ask if there's anything you can do. If they say no then you can walk to every office in the building and ask the same thing. If that doesn't work then you identify something and say, if the guy next to me works with Will Smith, then I'm going to go in there and say, I'm the biggest Will Smith fan in the world, is there anything I can help Will Smith on? Give me anything. That might generate an ok, do this. . . . You

do that with twenty different people and you may now have twenty different things to work on. So be a self-starter. You can't be reactive, you have to be active."

Nuñez reiterates that the biggest responsibility of an agent is to handle a client's career, and that can entail reading a script, discussing the story, negotiating a deal, solving a problem on an existing project, or planning what the next year is going to look like in terms of the films or projects that they should be involved with.

Nuñez says that CAA is a safe and supportive environment, unlike many agencies that are more competitive internally. Their philosophy is to be good to each other, and this is very important because working as an agent can be very stressful.

"When you are working with twenty clients, there is so much going on. . . . The stress, the volume of work, is really incredible, so you have to be able to handle stress, handle heavy workloads, handle a lot of things, and keep it all in motion. If I really stopped to think about everything that I'm doing, I could probably shock myself into some state of paranoia and depression. Into feeling it's so overwhelming, I could never do it. It's sort of like climbing a mountain. You just take one step at a time and eventually you get there.

"You have to be able to handle the pressure. You have to be able to keep a sense of balance in terms of the big picture, and you have to understand you are dealing with human beings, with artists that have issues. Everything that a client does is important to them because it's their life. You have to embrace the issue the same way. In order to be effective you have to make their issues your issues.

"You also have to be enthusiastic and identify with your clients. But you're not a cheerleader, you're a professional adviser. Yes, you must embrace and be passionate about the things that they are passionate about, but at the same time you have to have the objectivity and the future vision or view down the road to advise them correctly. Because it's personal to them and they may not be able to see all the issues down the road. That's my job. I have to be able to take something a client wants and explain to them why it is or is not good for them down the road."

Nuñez advises those wanting to break into this industry to refuse to let obstacles get in their way. "Once you know what you want to do within the industry, identify the goal with some general specificity. Pursue all the options that you can think of, and the caveat is that working at small companies might be easier to get into. They may offer a lot of hands-on experience, as opposed to going through a larger company where there may be a bureaucratic hierarchy. Be positive and work hard. Because in the beginning you may get paid very little and the hours may be very long, but if you stick with it, the rewards are great. And you end up doing a job you like and hopefully you'll get paid well for it."

Severo Perez, shown here in this film shoot, advises aspiring filmmakers to seek a broad education, develop skills that help in communication, and try to evolve with the ever-changing technology.

PART 3

Resources

Books and Organizations 86

Internet Resources 91

Master Index to Careers 92

Master Index to People Profiled 94

Index to this book 96

Books and Organizations

The American Film Institute. *Getting Started in Film*. New York: Prentice Hall, 1992.

Ball, William. *A Sense of Direction: Some Observations on the Art of Directing*. New York: Drama Book Publishers, 1984.

Berland, Terry, and Deborah Ouelette. *Breaking into Commercials: The Complete Guide to Marketing Yourself, Auditioning to Win, and Getting the Job*. New York: Penguin, 1997.

Blumenthal, Howard. *Careers in Television: You Can Do It!* Boston: Little, Brown, 1992.

Bly, Robert W. *Writers & Others Who Have a Way with Words*. Lincolnwood, IL: VGM Career Horizons, 1996.

Bone, Jan. *Opportunities in Film Careers*. Lincolnwood, IL: VGM Career Horizons, 1998.

Camenson, Blythe. *Careers in Writing*. Lincolnwood, IL: VGM Career Books, 2001.

Cooper, Donna. *Writing Great Screenplays for Film and TV: Learn the Art and Craft of Screenwriting from a Top Instructor at the AFI Film School*. 2nd edition. New York: Arco, 1997.

Cowfill, Linda J. *Writing Short Films: Structure and Content for Screenwriters*. Los Angeles: Lone Eagle Publishing Com., 1997.

Dougan, Pat. *Professional Acting in Television Commercials: Techniques, Exercises, Copy, and Storyboards*. Portsmouth, NH: Heinemann, 1995.

Engel, Joel. *Screenwriters on Screenwriting: The Best in the Business Discuss Their Craft*. New York: Hyperion, 1995.

Failde, Augusto, and William Doyle. *Latino Success: Insights from 100 of America's Most Powerful Latino Business Professionals*. New York: Simon and Schuster, 1997.

Field, Shelly. *100 Best Careers in Entertainment*. New York: Macmillan, 1995.

Field, Syd. *Screenplay: The Foundations of Screenwriting*. New York: Dell Publishing, 1994.

Goldberg, Jan. *Great Jobs for Theater Majors*. Linclolnwood, IL: VGM Career Horizons, 1998.

Javier, Frank, and Garcia Berumen. *The Chicano Hispanic Image in American Film*. New York: Vantage Press, Inc., 1995.

Kanner, Ellie, and Paul G. Bens, Jr. *NEXT! An Actor's Guide to Auditioning*. Los Angeles: Lone Eagle Publishing Co., 1997.

Kenig, Graciela. *Best Careers for Bilingual Latinos*. Lincolnwood, IL: VGM Career Books, 1999.

Mayfield, Katherine. *The Young Person's Guide to a Stage or Screen Career*. New York: Watson-Guptill Publications, 1998.

Millerson, Gerald. *Effective TV Production*. 3rd edition. Oxford: Focal Press, 1993.

The Minority Career Guide: What African Americans, Hispanics, and Asian Americans Must Know To Succeed in Corporate America. Princeton, NJ: Peterson's Guide, 1993.

Mogel, Leonard. *Careers in Communications and Entertainment.* New York: Simon & Schuster, 2000.

Noronha, Shonan. *Careers in Communications.* Lincolnwood, IL: VGM Career Horizons, 1997.

Reyes, Luis, and Peter Rubie. *Hispanics in Hollywood: An Encyclopedia of Film and Television.* Los Angeles: Lone Eagle Publishing Co., 2000.

Resnik, Gail, and Scott Trost. *All You Need to Know about the Movie and TV Business.* New York: Simon & Schuster, 1996.

Rivera, Miquela, Ph.D. *The Minority Career Book.* Holbrook, MA: Bob Adams, Inc., 1991.

Stevenson, Ollie. *The Colorblind Career: What Every African American, Hispanic American and Asian American Needs to Know to Succeed in Today's Tough Job Market.* Princeton, NJ: Peterson's Guides, 1997.

Stone, Vernon A. *Careers in Radio and Television News.* 7th edition. Washington, DC: Radio and Television News Directors Association, 1993.

What Can I Do Now? Preparing For a Career in Radio & TV. Chicago: Ferguson Publishing Company, 1998.

Periodicals

American Cinematographer. American Society of Cinematographers, P.O. Box 2230, Hollywood, CA 90078. 800-448-0145. www.cinematographer.com.

Backstage and *Backstage West.* 770 Broadway, New York, NY 10003. 646-654-5500. www.backstage.com.

Boxoffice Magazine. Suite 100, 6640 Sunset Boulevard, Hollywood, CA 90028. www.boxoff.com.

Broadcasting and Cable: The News Weekly of Television and Radio. 245 West 17 Street, New York, NY 10011. 212-645-0067. www.broadcastingcable.com

Electronic Media: The Programming Publication. 6500 Wilshire Boulevard, Suite 2300, Los Angeles, CA 90048. 323-370-2432. OR 711 Third Avenue, New York, NY 10017-4036. 212-210-0100. www.emonline.com

Hispanic. 999 Ponce de Leon, Suite 600, Coral Gables, FL 33134. 305-442-2462. www.hispaniconline.com

Journal of Popular Film and Television. 1319 18th Street NW, Washington, DC 20036-1802. 202-296-6267.

Lighting Dimensions. 32 West 18 Street, New York, NY 10011. www.lightingdimensions.com.

Media Week. 770 Broadway, 7th Floor, New York, NY 10003. 646-654-5125.

Premiere. 1633 Broadway, New York, NY 10019. 212-767-5400. www.premiere.com.

Television Quarterly. 111 West 57 Street, Suite 1020, New York, NY 10019. 212-586-8424.

Theatre Design and Technology. c/o Broadway Press, 3001 Springcrest Drive, Louisville, KY 40241-2765. 502-426-1211. www.broadwaypress.com/TDT/index.html

Variety. 5700 Wilshire Boulevard, Suite 120, Los Angeles, CA 90036-3659. 323-857-6600. www.variety.com.

Videomaker. Box 4591, Chico, CA 95927. 530-891-9009.

Financial Aid and Scholarship Publications, General

1999 Minority Guide to Scholarships and Financial Aid. Hampton, VA: Tinsley Communications, 1999.

American Legion Educational Program. *Need a Lift?* American Legion, National Emblem Sales, P.O. Box 1050, Indianapolis, IN 42206.

Bear, J., Ph.D. *Bear's Guide to Finding Money for College.* Berkeley, CA: Ten Speed Press, 1998.

Bruce-Young, D. *The Higher Education Moneybook for Women & Minorities.* Washington, DC: Enterprises International, Inc., 1996.

College Costs and Financial Aid Handbook, 1999. The College Entrance Examination Board, College Board Publications, Department WWW, 2 College Way, Forrester Center, WV 25438.

Dennis, M. J. *Barron's Complete College Financing Guide.* New York: Barron's Educational Series, Inc., 1999.

Leider, R., and A. Leider. *Don't Miss Out: The Ambitious Student's Guide to Financial Aid.* Alexandria, VA: A. Octameron Associates, 1999.

Peterson's College Money Handbook, 1999: Billions in Financial Aid. Peterson's Guides, P.O. Box 2123, 202 Carnegie Center Boulevard, Princeton, NJ 08543-2123.

Schlachter, G. A. *Directory of Financial Aids for Women.* Reference Service Press, P.O. Box 647, Richmond, CA 94808.

Schlachter, G. A., and R. D. Weber, eds. *Financial Aid for Hispanic Americans 1999–2001.* El Dorado Hills, CA: Reverence Service Press, 1999.

The Scholarship Handbook, 1999. The College Entrance Examination Board, College Board Publications, Department WWW, 2 College Way, Forrester Center, WV 25438.

Student Services L.L.C., Inc. *The Minority and Women's Complete Scholarship Book.* Naperville, IL: Sourcebooks Trade, 1998.

Financial Aid and Scholarship Programs for the Entertainment Industry

Ben Chatfield Scholarship, Radio and Television News Directors Foundation, 1000 Connecticut Avenue NW, Suite 615, Washington, DC 20036. 202-659-6510. www.rtnda.org.

The Broadcasting Training Program/ MIBTP (formerly the Minorities in Broadcasting Training Program), P.O. Box 1475, Santa Clarita, CA 91386-1475. 661-250-0080.

Directors Guild of America Student Film Awards, 7920 Sunset Boulevard, Los Angeles, CA 90046; 310-289-2000. www.dga.org.

Dow Jones Newspaper Fund Inc., *Journalism Career and Scholarship Guide*, P.O. Box 300, Princeton, NJ 08543-0300. 609-452-2820. www.dowjones.com/newsfund/home.html.

Inter American Press Association Scholarship Fund, 1801 SW 3rd Avenue, Miami, FL 33129. 305-285-7205. www.sipiapa.org.

The Museum of Television and Radio, (Los Angeles Branch) 465 North Beverly Drive, Beverly Hills, CA 90210. 310-786-1034. (New York City Branch) 25 West 52 Street, New York, NY 10019. (Both branches have internship programs). www.mtr.org.

National Association of Broadcasters, Broadcasting Research and Information Group, 1771 N Street NW, Washington, DC 20036-2891. 202-429-5380. www.nab.org/bcc/jobbank/scholarships.

Sundance Film Festival, 8857 West Olympic Boulevard, Suite 200, Beverly Hills, CA 90211-3605. 310-360-1981. www.sundance.org.

Scripps Howard Foundation Scholarships, P.O. Box 5380, 312 Walnut Street, 28th Floor, Cincinnati, OH 45201. 513-977-3035. www.scripps.com/foundation/index.html

William Randolph Hearst Foundation, 90 New Montgomery Street, Suite 1212, San Francisco, CA 94105-4504. 415-543-6033. www.fdncenter.org/grantmaker/hearst/awards.html

Professional Organizations and Associations

(Please note that many of these organizations offer scholarships and internships.)

Academy of Motion Pictures Arts and Sciences (AMPAS), 8949 Wilshire Boulevard, Beverly Hills, CA 90211-1972. 310-247-3000. www.oscars.org OR www.oscar.com.

Actors Equity Association, 165 West 46 Street, New York, NY 10036. 212-869-8530. www.actorsequity.org.

Affirmative Action Register, 8356 Olive Boulevard, St. Louis, MO 63132. 314-991-1335 or 800-537-0655. www.aar-eeo.com/

American Dance Guild, P.O. Box 2006, Lenox Hill Station, New York, NY 10021. 212-932-2789. www.americandanceguild.org.

American Federation of Television and Radio Artists (AFTRA), 260 Madison Avenue, New York, NY 10016. 212-532-0800. www.aftra.com.

American Film Institute, P.O. Box 27999, 2021 North Western Avenue, Los Angeles, CA 90027. 323-856-7600. OR The John F. Kennedy Center for the Performing Arts, Washington, DC 20566. 202-833-2348. www.afionline.org.

American Guild of Variety Artists, 184 Fifth Avenue, 6th Floor, New York, NY 10010. 212-675-1003.

The American Institute of Graphic Arts, 164 Fifth Avenue, New York, NY 10010. 212-807-1990. www.aiga.org.

American Society of Media Photographers, 150 North Second Street, Philadelphia, PA 19106. 215-451-2767. www.asmp.org.

Associated Actors and Artists of America, 165 West 46 Street, New York, NY 10036. 212-869-0358.

Association of Local Television Stations, 1320 19 Street NW, Suite 300, Washington, DC 20036. 202-887-1970. www.altv.com.

Association of Hispanic Arts, 260 West 26 Street, New York, NY 10001. 212-727-7227.

Broadcast Education Association, 1771 N Street NW, Washington, DC 20036-2891. 202-429-5354. www.beaweb.org

The California Chicano News Media Association, USC Annenberg School for Communication, 3502 Watt Way, ASC G38, Los Angeles, CA 90089-0281, 213-740-5263. www.ccnma.org.

Corporation for Public Broadcasting, Publications, 401 9 Street NW, Washington, DC 20004-2129. 202-879-9600. www.cpb.org.

ESPN, Inc., Human Resources Department, 935 Middle Street, Bristol, CT 06010. 860-585-2000. www.espn.com.

The Hispanic Alliance for Career Enhancement (HACE), 14 East Jackson Boulevard, Suite 1310, Chicago, IL 60604. 312-435-0498. www.hace_usa.org.

Hispanic Data, c/o Hispanic Business, 425 Pine Avenue, Santa Barbara, CA 93117. 805-964-4554. www.hispanicbusiness.com..

Hispanic Organization of Latin Actors (HOLA), Manuel Alfaro, Executive and Artistic Director, 107 Suffolk Street, Suite 302, New York, NY 10002. 212-253-1015. www.hellohola.org.

Intar Hispanic-American Arts Center, 508 West 53 Street, New York, NY 10019; P.O. Box 756, New York, NY 10108. 212-695-6134. intar@juno.com.

International Alliance of Theatrical Stage Employees, 1515 Broadway, Suite 601, New York, NY 10036. 212-730-1770. www.iatse.lm.com.

The International Media Center, 3000 NE 151 Street, North Miami, FL 33181. 305-919-5672. www.fiu.edu/~journal.

The International Radio and Television Society, 420 Lexington Avenue, Suite 1714, New York, NY 10170-0101. 212-867-6650. www.irts.org.

National Association of Broadcast Employees and Technicians (NABET), 501 3rd Street NW, 8th Floor, Washington, DC 20001. 800-882-9174. union.nabetcwa.org/nabet/.

National Association of Broadcasters, 1771 N Street NW, Washington, DC 20036-2891, 202-429-5300. www.nab.org/

National Endowment for the Arts, 1100 Pennsylvania Avenue NW, Room 617, Washington, DC 20506. 202-682-5400. arts.endow.gov.

New York Film Academy, 100 East 17 Street, New York, NY 10003. 212-674-4300. www.nyfa.com.

Producers Guild of America, 6363 Sunset Boulevard, 9th Floor, Hollywood, CA 90028. 323-960-2590. www.producersguild.com.

Puerto Rican Traveling Theatre, 304 West 47 Street, New York, NY 10019. 212-354-1293. www.prtt.org.

Radio-Television News Directors Association, 1000 Connecticut Avenue NW, Suite 615, Washington, DC 20036. 202-659-6510. www.rtnda.org.

Screen Actors Guild (SAG), 5757 Wilshire Boulevard, Los Angeles, CA 90036-3600. 323-954-1600. OR 1515 Broadway, New York, NY 10036. 212-44-1030. www.sag.com.

Society of Motion Picture and Television Engineers, 595 West Hartsdale Avenue, White Plains, NY 10607. 914-761-1100. www.smpte.org.

Teatro Pregones, 575 Walton Avenue, Bronx, New York 10451. 718-585-1202. www.pregones.org.

Theatre Communications Group (TCG),
355 Lexington Avenue, New York, NY
10017. 212-697-5230. www.tcg.org.

Women In Film, 8857 West Olympic Boulevard, Suite 201, Beverly Hills, CA
90211. 310-657-5144. www.wif.org/
home/index.html.

Internet
Resources

• •

Alliance for Community Media
www.alliancecm.org

Association for Education in Journalism
and Mass Communication

www.aejmc.sc.edu/AEJMC

Broadcast Employment Services

www.tvjobs.com

Hispanic American Theater

americantheater.about.com/
msubhispanic.htm

Hollywood Screenwriters Network

www.hollywoodnet.com/screennet.html

National Public Radio (NPR)

www.npr.org

Screenwriter Resources from the
Screenscribe

www.rt66.com/cedge/screen.htm

Screenwriters Online

www.screenwriter.com

World Radio Network

www.wrn.org/stations.html

Master Index to Careers

actor/actress, En
acupuncturist, SM
administrative assistant, CS, Ed
advertising copywriter, En
advertising salesperson, PC
agent, En, Sp, MI
agriculturalist, SM
alternative medical practitioner, SM
ambassador, LP
animator, En
archaeologist, SM
arranger/orchestrator, MI
art director, PC
associate director, nonprofit organization, CS
astronomer, SM
athlete, professional, Sp
athletic director, Sp
athletic trainer, Sp
attorney *see* lawyer
bailiff, LP
baseball umpire, Sp
biologist, SM
board member, CS
broadcast engineer, PC
broadcaster *see also* journalist, CS
bus driver, Ed
business owner, LE
casting director, En
chemist, SM
chief executive officer/executive director/president, CS, LE
chiropractor, SM
choreographer, En
cinematographer (director of photography), En
city administrator, LP
classified worker, Ed
coach/manager, Ed, Sp
columnist, PC

comedian, En
comedy writer, En
communications/media relations/public relations officer, CS
community affairs director (television), En
composer, En
computer engineer, Tc
computer programmer, Tc
computer technician, Tc
control room engineer, MI
copyeditor, PC
copyist, MI
copywriter, PC
costume designer (theater/television/film), En
court reporter, LP
crime prevention specialist, LP
criminal defense lawyer, LP
critic/reviewer, En, MI
data base manager, Tc
data entry clerk, Tc
data processing technician, Tc
dental hygienist, SM
dentist, SM
director (feature films or television), En
disc jockey/radio announcer, PC, MI
editor, PC
engineer, SM
engineering technician, SM
equipment manager, Sp
FBI agent, LP
film editor, En
fingerprint expert, LP
football referee, Sp
foreign service officer, LP
forester, SM
founder, CS, LE
fund-raiser for nonprofit organization, CS
general manager (station manager), PC

KEY
CS—Community Service
Ed—Education
En—Entertainment
LE—Latino Entrepreneurs
LP—Law and Politics
MI—Music Industry
PC—Publishing and Communications
SM—Science and Medicine
Sp—Sports
Tc—Technology

geologist, SM
government relations officer, LP
grant writer, CS
graphic designer, PC, Tc
graphics programmer, Tc
guidance counselor, Ed
home health care worker, CS
human rights worker, LP
immigration and customs officer, LP
instructional assistant, Ed
journalist, CS, En, LP, PC, Sp
judge, LP
justice of the peace, LP
juvenile detention officer, LP
labor representative (organizer, regional director), CS
laboratory technician, SM
lawyer (attorney, paralegal), CS, En, LP, Sp
    legal secretary, LP
librarian, Ed
lighting designer (theater), En
makeup artist (theater/television/film), En
manufacturer's representative, Sp
marketing director, Sp
medical doctor, CS, SM
medical scientist, SM
meteorologist/weather forecaster, PC, SM
news director, PC
news writer (radio), PC
notary public, LP
nurse, CS, SM
nutritionist, SM
optometrist, SM
paramedic, emergency medical technician (EMT), SM
parole officer, LP
personal manager, MI
personal trainer, Sp
pharmacist, SM
photographer or camera operator, PC
physical therapist, SM
physician, SM
physicist, SM
playwright, En
podiatrist, SM
police officer, LP
political lobbyist, LP
political strategist, LP
politician, LP
press agent, En

principal, Ed
probation officer, LP
producer, En
professional scout, Sp
professor, college or university, Ed
program director, PC
promoter, music and events, MI
proofreader, PC
psychiatrist, SM
psychologist, Ed, SM
public relations director, En, PC, Sp
publicist, Sp
publicity director, PC
publisher, PC
radio producer, PC
representative (Congress), LP
sales representative (books), PC
scenic designer (theater), En
science technician, SM
screenwriter, En
senator, LP
set designer (theater/television/film/video), En
singer, MI
songwriter, MI
sound editor, En
sports reporter/sportscaster, PC, Sp
stage director, En
stage manager, En
superintendent (school), Ed
systems analyst, Tc
teacher, Ed
    technical support specialist, Tc
technical writer, PC
television news anchor, PC
tour publicist, En
tuner, musical instruments, MI
translator/interpreter, LP
treaty negotiator, LP
veterinarian, SM
victim advocate, LP
Web master, Tc
writer, book, PC
youth coordinator, CS

Master Index to People Profiled

● ●

Acosta, Angela, Media Relations, Community Relations Director , CS

Acrivos, Juana Vivó, Professor of Chemistry, SM

Ahmed, Ada Diaz, founder and president of failed Latina Web site, Tc

Alonso, José Jr., Physicist, SM

Alvarado, Linda, Baseball Team Owner, Sp

Alvarez, Joe, Police Officer, Supervisor of Crime Stoppers, LP

Anaya, Rudolfo, Writer , PC

Ancira, Ernesto, Car Dealer, LE

Arellano, Jairo, Assistant Principal, Ed

Baca, Bettie, Senior Executive Service Candidate, LP

Baca, James, Mayor, LP

Barbosa, Pedro, Entomologist, SM

Barrientos, Gonzalo, State Senator, LP

Belli, Gioconda, Writer, PC

Benitez, John "Jellybean," disc jockey, recording artist, record producer, MI

Bezos, Jeff, founder and CEO of on-line store, Tc

Brown, Sarita, Educational Programs Administrator, Ed

Burr, Ramiro, music critic, MI

Cardona, Carlos, founder and senior vice president of Hispanic Web site, Tc

Carrera, Mario M., Senior Media Sales Executive, PC

Casillas, Ederlen, Codirector of nonprofit organization, CS

Centeno, Oscar, Business Owner, Trucking Company, LE

Chavez, Gabriel, Business Owner, Technology Company, LE

Cuellar, Henry, Secretary of State (Texas), LP

Davidds-Garrido, Norberto, professional football player, Sp

de la Hoya, Oscar, Professional Boxer, Sp

Del Olmo, Frank, Vice President of Professional Programs, CS

Del Toro, Benicio, Actor, En

Diaz, Freddy, graphic artist and graphic arts teacher, Tc

Diaz, Guadalupe "Aura," computer artist, Tc

Dominguez, Isabel, Geneticist, SM

Escalante, Jaime, Math Teacher, Ed, SM

Esparza, Moctesuma, Producer, En

Fernandez, Lisa, Softball Player, Sp

Flores, Tom, Football Coach, Sp

Galindo, Max, Paramedic, SM

Garcia, Abraham and Ana Corinna, Business Owners, Computer Company, LE

Garcia, Paul, Web master, Tc

Garcia, Rodolfo, Relationship Banker, LP

Gates, Ann Quiroz, computer science professor, Tc

Girón, Carlos, Sports Publicist, Sp

Gomez, Julio, founder and owner of e-commerce consulting firm, Tc

Gonzales, Enrique, project manager for a network of Web sites, Tc

Gonzales, Thomas, technology consultant, Tc

Gonzales, Victor, computer programmer, Tc

Gonzalez, Alex, Baseball Player, Sp

Gonzalez, Larry, Executive Director, LP

Guerrero, Lena, Political Lobbyist, LP

Gutiérrez, Margo, Librarian, Ed

Guzman-Macias, Estela, Special Education Teacher, Resource Specialist, Ed

Hayek, Salma Actress, En

Henley, Maria Jimenez, Stage Manager, Assistant Director, Choreographer, and Dancer, En

Hernandez, Antonia, Lawyer, President, CS

Hernandez, Fidel, Zoologist, SM

Hernandez, G. Herb, County Councilman at Large, LP

Hernandez-Castillo, Bel, Publisher, Editor-in-Chief, Dancer, and Actress, En

Herrera, Leticia, Business Owner, Cleaning Service, LE

Heumann, Judith, Assistant Secretary for Special Education, Ed

Jaime, Mental Health Technician, SM

Jimenez, James, City Administrator, LP

Kanellos, Nicolás, Book Publisher, PC

Leanos, John, Cultural Worker, Artist, LE

Leguizamo, John, Actor, Comedian, Playwright, En

Leoni, Dennis Edward, Writer, Producer, En

Llamosa, Carlos, Soccer Player, Sp
Llanos, Regla "Toni," dancer, choreographer, MI
Lopez, George, Comedian, En
Los Lobos (David Hidalgo, Conrad Lozano,
Louie Perez, and Cesar Rosas), musicians, MI
Martinez, Christine, radio disc jockey, MI
Martinez, Gilbert, Chief Judge, LP
Martinez, Rueben, Bookstore Owner, PC
Martinez, Walter, Magazine Publisher, Editor, PC
Massó, Jose, Center for the Study of Sport in
    Society, Sp
McBride, Theresa, computer systems consultant, Tc
Melendez, Bill, Animator, Producer, En
Mendoza, Araceli, Business Owner, Beauty Salon,
    LE
Mendoza, Graciela Contreras, Head Start Teacher,
    Ed
Monterroso, Benjamin, Labor Leader, CS
Morales, Dionicio, Founder and President, CS
Morales, Hugo, Radio Station Executive Director,
    PC
Moran, Julio, Executive Director of nonprofit
    organization, CS
Moreno, Richard Blackburn, President of nonprofit
    organization, CS
Moreno, Rita, Actress, Performer, En
Muniz, Marc Anthony, singer, MI
Nava, Gregory, Director, Writer, En
Nuñez, Emanuel, Agent, En
Nuñez, Tommy, Referee, Sp
O'Brien, Soledad, Television News Anchor, PC
Oceguera, Frank, III, Math Teacher, Ed
Olmos, Edward James, Actor, En
Ortega, Juan C., Design Firm President, Creative
    Director, PC
Ortega, Theresa, Veterinarian, SM
Penelas, Alex, Executive Mayor, LP
Perez, Lisandro, Sociology Professor, Ed
Perez, Pamela, Latino News Reporter, LP
Perez, Severo, Writer, Director, Producer, En
Porras-Field, Esperanza, Business Owner, Consulting
    Firm, Real Estate, LE
Portillo, Wendy, process control analyst, Tc
Ramirez, Eddie, promoter and event organizer, MI
Ramirez,Eddie, Promoter, event organizer, MI
Ramos, Jorge, Television News Anchor, PC
Rivas, Yolanda, manager of on-line software
    products, Tc
Roa, Horacio, practitioner of holistic medicine, SM
Rodriguez, Douglas, Chef and Restaurant Owner,
    LE

Rodriguez, Eloy, Toxicologist, SM
Rojas, Nydia, singer, MI
Romo, Ricardo, University President, Ed
Ruiz, John, Boxer, Sp
Sanchez, Guillermo, Dentist, SM
Sanchez, Josephine, Associate Director, CS
Sanchez, Loretta, Congresswoman, LP
Santana, Carlos, musician, MI
Santiago, Esmeralda, Writer, PC
Soto, Hilda Lorenia, e-commerce consultant, Tc
Tapia, Richard, Professor of Computational Applied
    Mathematics, SM
Tinjaca, Mabel, Author and Consultant in
    Organizational Development, LE
Tobar, Hector, National News Correspondent, PC
Trujillo, Gary, CEO of a failed Internet company,
    Tc
Vargas, Garrett, Software Design Engineer, PC
Vargas, Juan, Business Owner, Pinatas, LE
Villa, Brenda, Water Polo Player, Sp
Villalobos, Reynaldo, Cinematographer, Director,
    En
Wilkins, Ron, Probation Supervisor, LP
Yzaguirre, Raul, Executive Director of nonprofit
    organization, CS, LP
Zamora, Guadalupe, Family Doctor, SM
Zamora, Jim, Crime Scene Detective, LP
Zamora, Maria, Paraprofessional Educator, Ed

Index

Actor/Actress 14
Advertising Copywriter 14
Agent 16
Animator 16
Art Director/Production Designer 17
Attorney, Entertainment 17
Casting Director 17
Choreographer 18
Cinematographer 18
Comedian 21
Comedy Writer 21
Community Affairs Director (TV) 22
Composer 22
Costume Designer 23
Critic/Designer 23
Critic/Reviewer (Print Media) 23
Critic/Reviewer (TV/Radio) 23
Director (Feature Films) 25
Director (Television) 25
Esparza, Moctesuma
    birth of 39
    family 39
    early years 37, 39-40
    education 37-38, 40
Film Editor 26
Henley, Maria Jimenez
    birth of 44
    family 43-44,
    early years 44
    education 44-45
Hernandez-Castillo, Bel
    birth of 50
    family 50-51
    early years 50-51
    education 50-51
    Latin Heat 49-50, 53
Journalist, Entertainment 26
Leguizamo, John 20
Leoni, Dennis Edward
    birth of 55
    family 55
    early years 55
    education 55
    Lighting Designer (Theater) 27
Lopez, George
    birth of 62
    Cannes Film Festival 65
    DeBlasio, Ron (Mgr.) 63

    family 62
    early years 61-63
    education 62
    Morning Personality (Mega 92.3) 63
    Prinze, Freddie 63
Makeup Artist 27
Melendez, Bill
    birth of 67
    Disney, Walt 67-68
    family 67
    early years 67-68
    education 67-68
    Mendelson, Lee 67, 70
    Peanuts 67, 70-71
    Schulz, Charles 67, 70-71
Moreno, Rita 15
Nava, Gregory
    birth of 74
    Chavez, Cesar 75
    family 74-75
    early years 74-75
    education 74, 76
    Kahlo, Frida 75
    New Line Cinema 73
Nuñez, Emanuel
    birth of 79
    Creative Artists Agency 79, 81-82
    Estefan, Gloria 79
    family 79-80
    early years 79-80
    education 80-81
    International Creative Management 81
    Pacino, Al 79
Perez, Severo 24
Playwright 28
Press Agent, Personal 28
Press Agent, Theatrical 29
Producer 29
Public Relations and Promotional Director 30
Scenic Designer (Theater) 30
Screenwriter 30
Set Designer 31
Sound Editor 31
Stage Director (Theater) 32
Stage Manager (Theater) 32
Tour Publicist 32
Unit Publicist 33
Villalobos, Reynaldo 19